DATE			

© THE BAKER & TAYLOR CO.

Chaos on the Shop Floor

A Worker's View of Quality, Productivity, and Management

LABOR AND SOCIAL CHANGE
A series edited by Paula Rayman and Carmen Sirianni

CHAOS
on the Shop Floor

*A Worker's View of Quality, Productivity,
and Management*

Tom Juravich

TEMPLE UNIVERSITY PRESS
PHILADELPHIA

Temple University Press, Philadelphia 19122
© 1985 by Temple University. All rights reserved
Published 1985
Printed in the United States of America

Library of Congress Cataloging in Publication Data

Juravich, Tom.
   Chaos on the shop floor.

   (Labor and social change)
   Bibliography: p.
   Includes index.
   1. Quality of work life—United States—Case studies.
2. Industrial management—United States—Case studies.
I. Title.   II. Series.
HD6957.U6J87   1985   331.25   84-25279
ISBN 0-87722-375-0

For the women and men at National
and for my father

Contents

Acknowledgments

First and foremost, I must acknowledge the women and men whom I worked with at National Wire and Cable. I learned much more from them than I can convey in these pages. Their tenacity of will and ability to survive—where many would have given up—are not easily forgotten. No mere acknowledgment can fully repay my debt.

In addition to the workers at National, three people played important roles in this work. My partner, Marilyn McArthur, who was by far my harshest critic, was also my most ardent supporter. Michael Lewis was also a long-time supporter who saw the project through its various stages. Dan Clawson helped me work through many of the specific ideas; I benefited greatly from his interest.

My good friends Carole Counihan, Jordi Herold, D. Christopher Leonard, Judy Musket, and Elliot Soloway constantly encouraged me to complete this work. Our lively discussions over the years were invaluable. I would also like to thank Sara Ives and Charmaine Moore, who skillfully typed the manuscript. Although typing is often seen as a mindless technical operation, it was amazing to see the care they took with these pages.

Finally, a word of thanks to Michael Ames of Temple University Press and Carmen Sirianni, co-editor of the Labor and Social Change series. Their belief in this project helped bring it to fruition.

Chaos on the Shop Floor

A Worker's View of Quality, Productivity, and Management

1. Introduction

UNTIL RECENTLY THE UNITED STATES maintained an almost unquestioned superiority in industrial manufacturing. Not only were American products seen as superior, but our production methods were regarded as the finest and most innovative. American manufacturing supplied the model for the rest of the world. In recent years, however, we have seen American manufacturing fall to a level unthinkable even ten years ago. American products have lost their world prominence, and our production methods now seem the antiquated remnants of an earlier era. This decline has spurred a variety of explanations (and solutions) for the fall from grace. These recommendations have ranged from pleas for making more capital available for businesses (Peterson, 1982); to calls for federal legislation (Magaziner and Reich, 1983); to demands for concessions by trade unions (Drucker, 1981); and to more systematic critiques of the economy (Bowles et al., 1983).

Underlying these various analyses is a concern with two focal issues: the quality of our products, and the decline in productivity of our factories and workforces. Yet despite the magnitude of the available literature, workers' views of what is wrong with American manufacturing are almost entirely absent from the debate. Because of their intimate connection with the manufacturing process, workers would seem to have much to contribute. Yet somehow they have been ignored. That they are so often blamed for our problems with quality and productivity makes it doubly important that their views be heard.

Studies that at least attempt to consider workers' views rely

Introduction

primarily on Studs Terkel's *Working* (1972) and HEW report *Work in America* (1973). Although both are important, they are based on research conducted at least fifteen years ago, considerably before the crisis in manufacturing became acute. There is a less well-known ethnographic literature of the industrial workplace (Cavendish, 1982; Linhart, 1981; Pfeffer, 1979; Schrank, 1978), but it tends to be concerned with painting general portraits of workers.

Because the literature on our industrial crisis has generally failed to investigate workers' perspectives, it has relied on conventional views of industry and industrial workers. As we will see, these conventional views are only partly accurate

Contemporary Views of the Industrial Workplace

Perhaps the most important conventional assumption about the industrial workplace concerns the nature of industrial work. It is generally assumed that the contemporary industrial workplace involves little (if any) skilled work. Gone are the days of the skilled craftsman who followed a product through various stages of production. Instead, modern industry has broken jobs into their smallest components, with workers performing a single task over and over. As described by Phil Stallings, a spot welder interviewed by Studs Terkel,

> I stand in one spot, about a two-or-three foot area, all night. The only time a person stops is when the line stops. We do about thirty-two jobs (welds) per car, per unit. Forty-eight units an hour, eight hours a day. Thirty-two times forty-eight times eight. Figure it out. That's how many times I push that button (Terkel, 1972: 221–22).

6

In this fashion, the millions of motions necessary to produce an automobile have been reduced to a large number of simple, repetitive tasks, an organization of the workplace that represents the rationality of the engineer and the manager. Although such a rationalized system represents a scientific and technical form of industrial assembly, most of us shudder at the consequences it has for Phil Stallings or for us, if we were in his place.

Recognizing that most industrial work is so subdivided and segmented makes it difficult to believe that such work requires much skill. How much ability does it take to push the button on a welder 12,288 times per night? Jobs like Phil Stallings' seem to require grim determination rather than skill.

This brings us to a second conventional assumption about the industrial workplace. Given jobs like Phil Stallings', it suggests that workers tolerate their jobs at best, and that many actively hate them. According to the HEW report, "Significant numbers of American workers are dissatisfied with the quality of their working lives. Dull, repetitive, seemingly meaningless tasks, offering little challenge or autonomy" (HEW, 1973: xv). As Nora Watson expressed it, "Most of us, like the assembly line worker, have jobs that are too small for our spirit. Jobs are not big enough for people" (Terkel, 1972: xxix).

The conventional wisdom accepts the premise that most industrial jobs "aren't big enough for people," and also the conclusion that follows: "As a result, the productivity of the workers is low—as measured by absenteeism, turnover rates, wildcat strikes, sabotage, poor quality products, and a reluctance by workers to commit themselves to their work tasks" (HEW, 1973: xvi). The recognition that this phenomenon was widespread led HEW to recommend massive "job humanization" programs. Essentially the same ar-

Introduction

gument can be found in Simmons and Mares' *Working Together* (1983), which was written ten years later.

A third characteristic of the industrial workplace is much less widely discussed. It comes largely out of a more specialized literature on the labor process, much of which is written from a Marxist perspective. Its major emphasis is how the modern industrial workplace is designed not only to maximize profits, but to control workers as well.[1] For example, David Noble argues that numerically controlled machine tools were chosen over other options in the machine tool trade because they deskilled more workers, thereby reducing worker control over production (Zimbalist, 1979: 18–50). Thus the domination of workers in the workplace itself is perceived as highly rational and planned. As Harry Braverman writes in his seminal work, *Labor and Monopoly Capital,*

> The concept of control adopted by modern management requires that every activity in production have its several parallel activities in the management center: each must be devised, precalculated, tested, laid out, assigned and ordered, checked and inspected and recorded throughout its duration and completion (Braveman, 1974: 125).

According to Braverman, domination is not haphazard or occasional, but is quite systematic in character and evidenced in virtually every management decision.

1. See Harry Braverman, *Labor and Monopoly Capital* (New York: Monthly Review Press, 1974); David F. Noble, *America by Design* (New York: Oxford University Press, 1977); Andrew Zimbalist, ed., *Case Studies on the Labor Process* (New York: Monthly Review Press, 1979); Joan M. Greenbaum, *In the Name of Efficiency* (Philadelphia: Temple University Press, 1979); and Dan Clawson, *Bureaucracy and the Labor Process* (New York: Monthly Review Press, 1980).

National Wire and Cable Company

A fourth characteristic, implicit in the first three, is the belief that most industrial workers are employed in large plants. An auto worker like Phil Stallings, who performs repetitious tasks under direct supervision, represents the archetype.

These four characteristics—the deskilled nature of industrial work, workers' dislike of this work, their systematic domination by management, and the large size of industrial plants—create the contemporary image of the industrial workplace. Unfortunately for the industrial worker, this view contains much truth. Yet like all stereotypes, it is overly simplistic. If the ethnographic studies by Terkel (1972) and Garson (1975) tell us anything, it is that the world of work is more diverse than usually assumed.

I hope in this present work to offer some insights as to how this conventional view needs to be altered. I would like now to turn to the case study that informs this inquiry.

National Wire and Cable Company[2]

To gain a worker's perspective on our present industrial crisis, I went to work as a mechanic for the National Wire and Cable Company in the fall of 1980. Located in the factory section of a New England city of 50,000, National was a locally owned, nonunion company that employed approximately 150 workers. It produced three kinds of products, which corresponded roughly to the three floors of the mill. On the first floor it manufactured a special kind of insulated electrical wire that is used in situations of extreme temperature. The floor resembled a textile mill more than a wire mill, with rows of braiding machines that wove dacron jackets over

2. This as well as all other names have been changed.

Introduction

strained copper wire. Despite the large size of this operation, it employed a relatively small and stable workforce, mostly composed of men.

Some of this wire was shipped directly to corporate customers, but much of it was used as raw material on the second floor, where I worked. Although we performed a number of small jobs that involved cutting, stripping, and placing terminals (connectors) on conventional plastic-coated wire to fabricate wire harnesses, our major product was a three-wire assembly made from our own wire.[3] This involved twenty to forty women doing simple assembly work to produce thousands of these assemblies each day. The work was boring at best. National operated essentially as a subcontractor, producing large numbers of these assemblies for two major corporations who used them in appliances. Ours was a very specialized product, generally unsalable on the open market.

Like many other companies, National had moved into the high-tech market, the third floor producing computer cables and connectors. As on the second floor, this involved twenty to forty women doing routine assembly. Their work largely entailed soldering multiple connectors on the ends of multiconductor cables. These very specialized cables were made for two large high-tech manufacturers.

There was a complete sexual division of labor at National. All the women worked in assembly positions, while the men held the

---

3. To facilitate faster assembly of electric and electronic products, a wire harness is used rather than individually measuring, cutting, and fastening electrical components together. It usually consists of a number of different colored wires that are precut and ready for fast assembly and that have a number of terminals (connectors) and other connecting devices. The most common wire harness is used under the dashboard of your car.

semiskilled and supervisory positions. All positions, however, were low paid. The women began at minimum wage (at that time $3.35 per hour), and increases were slow and in small increments ($.10 to $.15 over three to four months). Other positions were also poorly paid, with the head mechanic making only $5.50 per hour. (This salary represented one-half of what the head mechanic earned in a large unionized mill in the same town.)

The combination of poor pay, boring work and (as we shall see) confusion on the job contributed to a high turnover rate. In any given month close to one-third of the workers were new. The pay and conditions also forced down the age of the work force. The majority were under twenty-five, with only a handful over thirty-five. Also, in a city that was 40 per cent Hispanic, all employees were white.

National belongs to what is called the "periphery" of manufacturing, or the "secondary labor market" (Doeringer and Piore, 1971; Gordon, 1972; Edwards, Reich, and Gordon, 1975). Although this view has undergone refinements (see Gordon, Edwards, and Reich, 1982), it essentially argues that there are two types of manufacturing firms and consequently two distinct labor markets. The "core" consists of large, stable firms in which workers can expect long-term employment. General Motors and IBM, for example, are core firms. The periphery, on the other hand, consists of small, relatively unstable firms. Larger firms depend on these to take the risks of some kinds of production and inventory. "In peripheral firms where product demand was unstable, jobs tended to be marked by instability; therefore workers in the secondary labor market experienced higher turnover rates" (Edwards, Reich, and Gordon, 1975: xv). Although some companies may fall on the dividing line between types of firms, National is clearly part of the "periphery."

Introduction

Small Shop, Large Shop

Our description of National thus far seems very different from the manufacturing that takes place in large plants. Moreover, as large multinationals increasingly dominate production, small shops would seem even more a part of the past, and hardly important in our contemporary discussions of our manufacturing crisis.

Yet this stereotype is misleading. As reported in the U.S. *Census of Manufacturers* (1977), 43.3 per cent, almost half of the workers in U.S. manufacturing, are in firms that employ fewer than 250 people. Granovetter (1984) presents a startling finding: "While there can be no doubt that large corporations have increased in importance during this century . . . the size of the workplace has hardly changed since 1920" (Granovetter, 1984: 323).

Futhermore, there is every indication that small shops will grow in number. Before the widespread use of computers and data processing equipment, it made sense to keep production centralized. Now, however, it is possible to link small plants in different locations by computer, which can create savings due to availability of materials and labor (Earl, 1981: 356-66). This ability to utilize low paid workers in many geographic locations has been responsible for the flight of many factories to the Sunbelt and right-to-work states (Bluestone and Harrison, 1982). The degree to which our economy slides toward "service" and "information" also favors smaller and decentralized workplaces (Plewes, 1982: 7-15).

In addition (although information is scanty), there appears to be a growth in subcontracting, especially within the high-tech industry (Bluestone and Harrison, 1982). Rather than perform all the tasks of a given product line, the parent company subcontracts the more labor-intensive tasks to firms like National. In fact, our three-wire assembly had previously been manufactured in-house by the companies that now subcontracted them to us.

Small Shop, Large Shop

Subcontracting is extremely common among Japanese firms, and it affects the size of their shops (Woronoff, 1983; Scott-Stokes, 1982; Molony, 1982). As Granovetter reports, "Whereas the typical proportion of workers in U.S. manufacturing plants of less than 100 employees has hovered around 25% for much of this century, the comparable Japanese figure has been much closer to 50%" (Granovetter, 1984: 330). As American companies continue to follow the Japanese lead, we can expect both subcontracting and the number of small companies like National to grow. Thus, small shops will continue to be a part of the American industrial landscape.

The small shop has gone unnoticed not only in the conventional wisdom, but in industrial literature as well. From the early works of Mayo (1933) through Chinoy (1955) and Braverman (1974), the fascination has been with large industrial mills. Granovetter concurs: "If we take the distribution of labor market research locations as an indicator of implicit assumptions, we would have to conclude that conservative and radical writers alike . . . have assumed the typical worker to reside in a large manufacturing establishment with at least one thousand workers" (Granovetter, 1984: 324). Not only has this emphasis failed to address the millions of workers in small shops, it makes it easier to overlook some aspects of industrial work which happen to be more visible in small shops. Indeed, this focus on the large industrial workplace is in part responsible for the conventional overly rational image of industrial work. From this, the conventional view concludes that the problems of the workplace and industry (poor quality, low productivity, job indifference) result from over-rationalization. The present study arrives at quite different conclusions.

Like Phil Stallings, the people at National performed work that was hardly exciting. Most of them, like the women on my floor, performed repetitive, simple operations thousands of times each

Introduction

day. At first glance, then, National appears to conform to our conception of the typical industrial workplace. Yet, upon further inspection, some important differences emerge. First, although most work at National was repetitive, it was less automatic and routine than the stereotype suggests. Phil Stallings gives the impression that his work goes on continually, that he simply presses the button on his welder hour upon hour. What I saw at National, however, was a great deal of confusion and chaos even in very simple jobs: procedures were changed, machines broke down, poor materials were pushed through the line. Much of this confusion resulted from decisions made by management. Most decisions were made for the short run, without long-term goals in mind. But more than that, some decisions seemed to have no goal at all and could only be perceived as "bad" decisions. Thus, although the stereotype portrays the industrial workplace as the epitome of rationalization (in fact over-rationalization), it was surprising to learn how confused a shop could be.

Rather than proceeding automatically, production at National constantly encountered a number of obstacles. When these obstacles (poor materials, ill-repaired machines) arose, a specialized kind of knowledge was required, quite different from that normally needed to perform the job. It was especially then, in their encountering and overcoming these obstacles, that I discovered that experienced workers possessed a surprising amount of craft knowledge. In the case of Phil Stallings, for example, it first appears that his speed results entirely from the rationality of his work situation. Yet my findings suggest that his speed also results from his ability to deal with difficulties as if they never arose.

Besides observing the irrationality of production at National and the need of workers to develop craft knowledge to overcome these obstacles in production, I also uncovered an unexpected source of worker discontent. The conventional explanation has it that the division of jobs into small and meaningless tasks is the primary factor behind worker dissatisfaction. Hence the stress on job humanization programs. I do not deny there is much truth in this position. However, if the industrial workplace is not as rational as we have assumed, then it is important to inquire into other sources of this dissatisfaction.

In contrast to our conventional wisdom, I was surprised to discover how much pride the workers at National took in what appeared to be meaningless tasks. Although most of the jobs were essentially trivial, I observed workers making them meaningful in order to survive. As Barbara Garson writes, "Somehow in the unending flow of parts and papers, with operations subdivided beyond any recognizable unit of accomplishment, people still find ways to define certain stacks of work as 'theirs'; certain piles as 'today's' and 'tomorrow's' " (Garson, 1975: xi).

As I witnessed at National, dissatisfaction stemmed not only from the rationality of the mill, but from the irrationality of production, particularly when obstacles prevented workers from enjoying what little pride they could create out of their jobs. Given the chaos that resulted from poor management decisions, it is surprising that workers cared about their work at all.

The recognition of a considerable amount of irrationality in the industrial workplace also forces us to reconsider the ways in which domination operates in the workplace. There were distinct tendencies at National toward the increased control of workers through segmentation of tasks. Yet imperfect management control (aided by lack of competence) rendered this tendency less systematic than the conventional view would have us believe. As Goldhaber (1980) has suggested, Braverman may have been overzealous in his deskilling argument: "Harry Braverman insightfully depicted the

Introduction

role of technology in routine work and controlling workers. Mesmerized by this analysis, the left has failed to examine the enormous diversity of technological practice and the potentially *destabilizing* effect of technical practice" (Goldhaber, 1980: 13 [emphasis added]).

In fact, it is surprising how little control National's management really exercised. Most aspects of production were extremely haphazard and had never been tested or planned. They had evolved out of workers' "folk practices," not management design. This constant shop floor confusion also blocked the production of quality items at a regular pace, which damaged worker morale. It simultaneously created an unpredictable work environment, thereby undercutting workers' attempts to devise strategies of survival.

Less Than Rational Workplaces

This brief summary suggests that there are important differences between the small shop and the large industrial workplace. This is especially true of the degree to which the workplace has been rationalized. There are a number of reasons why smaller shops tend to be more disorganized. First, the scale of most small shops simply does not allow for the routinization of production procedures to become so mechanized. When production only involves a few workers producing small numbers of an item for a few days, it does not make sense to plan each part of the process in advance. Instead, production tends to proceed on an ad hoc basis, with the worker taking primary responsibility. This was the case in National for many of our smaller jobs.

Even on our larger production lines, like the manufacture of the three-wire assembly, there was considerable looseness. As we will see, despite management's desire to tighten up production, because of a lack of a trained staff, things never seemed to change. Unlike most large mills, we had no engineering department and only one time-study person for the whole plant.

In addition, most workers at National performed a number of jobs as demand increased in one area and fell in another. Without a union contract or clear job descriptions, and augmented by this shift in demand, workers did not know from day to day what they would be doing. This added to the confusion on the floor and hindered workers from becoming experienced at any one job.

Thus a number of tendencies in the small shop encouraged an ad hoc style of production. Unfortunately, small is not always beautiful, especially when applied to industrial workplaces. Not that Phil Stallings has it easy, but in many ways the workers at National had it worse. They suffered boredom like Phil, but with more confusion, while earning only one-third as much.[4]

There is growing evidence that what I found at National may not be restricted to small shops. Literature from three separate areas suggests that irrationality in the production process is more prevalent than the conventional wisdom suggests. I would like to look briefly at these three bodies of literature, to illustrate that what I observed at National is part of larger tendencies in American industry.

We already noted that much of the shop-floor confusion at National was a function of short-term planning. Since the publication of Hayes and Abernathy's seminal "Managing Our Way to Economic Decline" (1980), a host of articles by managers them-

---

4. This is based on the average wage of an auto worker, which was $12.00 per hour according to the *United Auto Workers Research Bulletin* (September–October 1982).

Introduction

selves have leveled similar criticisms of American industry. As Hayes and Abernathy put it, "Our managers still earn generally high marks for their skill in improving short-term efficiency, but their counterparts in Europe and Japan have started to question America's entrepreneurial imagination and willingness to make risky long-term competitive decisions" (Hayes and Abernathy, 1980: 68).

The critique by the business community goes beyond complaints of inadequate long-term planning. In a recent issue of the *Harvard Business Review*, Arnold Judson (1982) argues that much of our drop in productivity is simply a result of poor management decisions: "The scope of most productivity improvements is too narrow. Their focus is primarily—and often exclusively—on cost savings in one or another part of a company, not even thoughout the company as a whole" (Judson, 1982: 94).

Consequently, production in large firms often ends up as confused as at National. John DeLorean, for example, recounts startling evidence of shop-floor irrationalities at General Motors:

> One was the totally inefficient use of Chevrolet's manufacturing plants because there was no way to coordinate material control with sales orders. When a new-car order was placed with the dealer, it sat for ten days to two weeks until there was time available in a production plant: It was then read to see if the car ordered by the dealer could be actually built. (As many as 30 percent of all new-car orders have errors, such as a dealer mistakenly ordering a Nova with an engine which is not available for that car line.) If the order was correct, it was put into the production schedule. If it wasn't, it was kicked back to the dealer for correction and then sent back to the corporation where it sat for another ten days to two weeks before it was read a second time. If it was wrong again, it went through the whole process a third or fourth time if necessary (Wright, 1979: 122–23).

Less than Rational Workplaces

DeLorean reports numerous examples of poor management planning. In another, he recalls that when he took over the Chevrolet division there were 2,720 possible dashboard combinations for a single model, the Camaro.

Other literature suggests parallels between the problems of the small shop and those of larger industries. Recent ethnographies by Cavendish (1982), Linhart (1981), and to some degree those of Garson (1975) and Pfeffer (1979) confirm the shop-floor irrationality caused by short-term planning in large industrial workplaces. Indeed, in many the workplaces they describe resemble what I observed at National. For example, few if any of National's workers received any training for their jobs. Cavendish (1982) and Linhart (1981) describe the same system—or lack of system—in the large industrial mills where they worked. "When you were learning a new job, Margaret, the training woman, demonstrated it once, then went away and left you to do it" (Cavendish, 1982: 20). Thus our conventional view of the rational workplace in part reflects the distance from which industry is often observed. From the vantage point of the shop floor, a great deal of the "rationality" melts into chaos and confusion.

A third relevant body of literature attempts to link issues of productivity and quality with more general issues of the American economy (Bluestone and Harrison, 1982; Bowles et al., 1983; The Institute for Labor Education and Research, 1982; Melman, 1983). The most systematic work on this subject is Bowles, Gordon, and Weisskopf's *Beyond the Waste Land* (1983). In what amounts to an innovative approach to the economic system, they argue that declines in our productivity and standard of living have been caused not by a shortage of capital to invest or by unproductive workers, but by waste: "The U.S. economy falls far short of its productive potential, squandering time, energy, and natural resources on a

19

Introduction

monumental scale" (Bowles, Gordon, and Weisskopt, 1983: 4). As we shall see, National is in many ways a case study in waste. If we are to "reclaim" the waste land, the wasteful tendencies throughout American industry will have be recognized and dealt with.

Researcher as Participant

Before proceeding, it is important to discuss the methods employed in this research. Because we typically think of researchers as studying "others," it is especially important to outline how this research was conducted while I was an active participant.

There are certainly other ways to investigate workers' views of our current industrial crisis. The most common would be to administer a questionnaire. The basic premise of this kind of research is that by carefully choosing a representative (typical) sample, findings can be generalized to the entire group—in this case, workers (Wallace, 1971). Its goal is to be able to make general statements which apply to all workers. I have strong reasons, however, for choosing a different strategy.

The first is my belief that the world of shop-floor workers is so different from the middle-class professional world that it is difficult to understand without first-hand experience. In this sense, it is extremely difficult for survey researchers to know what kind of questions to ask or even how to frame questions properly. Second, my decision to become a shop-floor worker stems from my belief that industrial life cannot be understood by a static snapshot or broad generalizations. Instead, I would argue that the "reality" of industrial life lies in its everyday, mundane details. Although I could have interviewed industrial workers during or after work, I would have missed much of what Geertz (1973) calls the "thickness" of everyday life.[5]

This kind of participant observation has a long sociological tradition.[6] However, because this method is by its nature somewhat idiosyncratic, I would like to outline my particular approach. The research falls into three basic stages. My first goal was to learn to see events in the mill as workers do. It is not that I became exactly like those who worked in the mill in all senses, but that I was able to see everyday events in their terms. The second stage was to go beyond simply interpreting discrete events as a worker, and begin the sociological task of linking these events together, in some sense critically. At this point I left the "data" per se, and began the theoretical part of this analysis.

Because the term "theory" has so many meanings in the social sciences, it is important to clarify my usage. In the classical sense, theory refers to philosophic and abstract analyses of issues and

5. In this sense, this work is in the tradition of "interpretive social science." See Peter Winch, *The Idea of a Social Science* (London: Routledge and Kegan Paul, 1958); Robert Borger and Frank Cioffi, eds., *Explanation in the Behavioral Sciences* (Cambridge, Eng.: Cambridge University Press, 1970); Clifford Geertz, *The Interpretation of Culture* (New York: Basic Books, 1973); and Paul Rabinow and William M. Sullivan, eds., *Interpretive Social Science* (Berkeley: University of California Press, 1979).

6. For a discussion of the origins of participant observation in American sociology, see: John Madge, *The Origins of Scientific Sociology* (New York: Free Press, 1962); and Martin Bulmer, *The Chicago School of Sociology: Institutionalization, Diversity, and the Rise of Sociological Research* (Chicago: University of Chicago Press, 1985). For a discussion of the methods of participant observation, see: Norman K. Denzin, ed., *Sociological Methods: A Sourcebook* (Chicago: Aldine, 1970); and Robert Bogdan and Steven J. Taylor, *Introduction to Qualitative Research Methods* (New York: John Wiley & Sons, 1975).

Introduction

events. This is what Mills (1959) aptly termed "grand theory." More recently, under the rubric of "middle range theory" (Merton, 1949), the term has come to mean a set of logically related propositions in some testable form. I see the theoretical aspects of this work in neither of those two traditions, but instead view it as what has been called "grounded theory" (Glaser and Strauss, 1967). In other words, the theory does not have roots in an abstract philosophical system nor in a logical deductive system, but is rooted in my practical experience in the mill.

The second stage of the research is theoretical in that it takes the specific incidents and events from the shop floor and links them together critically. It is grounded in the case study, yet it is theoretical and speculative in that it goes beyond specific details. In this sense it attempts to make a whole out of disparate parts.

In the third stage of research I not only link together events and issues of the workplace, but relate them to larger external issues. Here I use not only my mill experience but relevant literature to depict the contemporary workplace from a worker's perspective. Again, it is grounded in my field experience, but attempts to situate that experience in contemporary concerns. It is through the theoretical aspects of this research that I hope to broaden my conclusions beyond those available from the specific empirical case. I am not suggesting that I can generalize from this specific case to industrial workers in general, but it is my hope that by articulating and following through some of the implications from my experiences at National, it will begin to open up dialogue on a neglected issue in our industrial crisis.

2. In the Mill

PERHAPS THE BEST WAY TO INTRODUCE
the mill is to describe my first few weeks on the job. While I was
still new, I tended to be much more observant since I saw National
with "outsider's" eyes, much like the reader. As I stayed longer at
National, I lost this freshness and began to see things more like a
National worker. Although I cannot recount even a majority of the
mill's activities, I have tried to select those that suggest what it was
like.

The mechanic's job I had taken was ideal for getting to know the
mill. Unlike most workers, I was not tied to a single location or
machine. So despite being busy during my first weeks, I was able to
gain a good general view of the mill's operation. As I became more
proficient at my own job, I was able to widen my understanding.

Because my job was to repair and set up machines for specific
tasks, I was more aware than most production workers of how the
machinery, in many ways, forms the basis of the production process. A discussion of these machines offers a good introduction to
the operations at National. Indeed, the chaos on the shop floor
begins at precisely this point.

On the Job

It was not without trepidation that I walked onto the floor the first
morning. It didn't help that the first comment I met was, "The
shift starts at 7, not 8" (I had been in the personnel office, filling
out forms). Although I had worked in a variety of different mills for

In the Mill

a total of three years, that had been five years ago. To make matters worse, I had taken a job as a machine mechanic (or what is called a maintenance position in the mills), a job I had never actually performed. I had worked occasionally on machines in other jobs, and have worked with tools for much of my life. But I lacked the experience I had indicated on my application. To put it frankly, I was terrified of being "found out" and promptly fired.

After my arrival on the floor, I was taken back to work with Bobby. I had been introduced to him three days earlier while being interviewed. He was already "elbow up" in grease, working on one of two large machines in the back of the floor. The number of people who came by in white coats and suits during the course of the morning made it clear that these machines were important. I learned later that they produced the basic material upon which the floor depended. Neither was running that morning.

Like most people on their first day of work, I had no idea what to do. I seemed to be in Bobby's way everywhere I stood. I wanted to show him I was eager to learn, but he scowled if I peered too closely at what he was doing. In truth, he had good reason to scowl, because I had been hired as his boss. My own boss (his official title was production manager) was named Carroll, a thin, wiry, nervous man in his late 40s. Carroll was dissatisfied with Bobby's work. Impressed by my college background (I indicated some college experience on my job application), he kept repeating that "Bobby just doesn't have the knowledge to do the job." So I was hired to glean what I could from Bobby, and by a month's end become his supervisor. Carroll had told Bobby all this just that morning, which explained why he wasn't very friendly.

While I watched, Bobby made adjustments on one of the machines. Although I had learned from past experience never to accept a boss's evaluation blindly, I remember being unimpressed with Bobby's skills. Not that I had the slightest idea of what to do, but the way he carried himself suggested less than competence. Although not yet twenty years old, he displayed none of the youthful self-confidence common to many men his age. He was withdrawn, and his eyes were constantly darting around as if someone were watching him. He also moved with hesitancy. Yet he was not slow; in fact, although he was slightly built, I was surprised to discover that he was quite strong. Yet there was an uncertainty about his movements.

Bobby was working on one of two almost identical "Single End Lead Machines." We called them SELMs, although it was months before I realized that the term was an acronym. They were the size of a compact car, with an assembly that fed wire extending twelve feet perpendicular to the main body of the machine. These machines cut a wire to length, stripped both ends and applied a terminal (a connector) to one end (hence *Single* End Lead Machine). However, the terminals were not going on correctly that morning, and were smashing in the machine.

Bobby eventually explained that he was adjusting the mechanism that applied the "terms" as he called them (an abbreviation for terminals). They were supplied by a large continuous reel that hung above the machine. The mechanism inserted a terminal around the stripped end of a wire (which was advanced by a conveyor), and with a crash that shook both the machine and the floor cut the terminal off the reel and crimped it around the wire. This happened every two seconds.

We worked through coffeebreak, or more accurately, Bobby worked while I watched. I felt a little better when he showed me what was wrong. The terminal was not advancing enough and

In the Mill

therefore was being cut off too soon. When it was crimped, it smashed the terminals. Bobby continued to tinker when Carroll, whose office was upstairs, came down to see how we were coming.

Carroll had a number of ideas about what was wrong. He pointed to the "foot" that advanced the strip of terminals, which we had been adjusting all morning, and told Bobby that he shouldn't have touched it. "It's a very sensitive adjustment and once you get it right, mark it so this never happens again." Bobby tried a few more adjustments, but instead of getting better, it got worse. At that point Carroll took the screwdriver out of Bobby's hand and turned the screw in the opposite direction. No matter how far he turned it, it didn't get better. He was trying another adjustment when he was paged over the intercom. As he was leaving, he turned to me and said, "Remember what I told you about that foot. Once you get it set, mark it and then leave it alone."

We went back to Bobby adjusting while I watched. We were both stunned by Carroll's behavior, although in different ways. I had seen bosses give workers verbal abuse, but touching another man's tools is a serious violation of shop-floor practices. I had witnessed blows over a similar incident in another plant. Visibly shaken, Bobby was less angry than insulted. "What does he think I am . . . some kind of dummy? He had no idea of what to do." In the coming months, Bobby would repeat that phrase, "What does he think I am?" over and over. It was probably more descriptive of Carroll's attitude toward the workers at National than anything else I heard during my stay.

I was momentarily drawn away from the SELM when one of the women asked me to look at a machine she said was smoking. I walked over, hoping I could figure out what was wrong. Sure enough, smoke was spewing from it. When I tried to start the machine, something was binding and it hardly ran. Carroll, who was back on the floor, pointed out the problem: "Clean that bar off good with emory cloth and give it a good oiling." It took me half an hour to find the emory cloth (typical for the first day on the job), and I was so scared of scoring (stratching) this perfectly square metal bar that I hardly touched it with the emory cloth. I did give it a good oiling, though, and it ran fine for the rest of the day.

Meanwhile, Bobby had been able to get the SELM running. Each time the slack on the reel of terminals tightened up, however, the machine pulled the reel and the terminals smashed. A number of these smashed terminals jammed in the applicator and broke the blade that cut them off. I watched as Bobby removed the entire applicator (approximately the size of a brick) which was easily detachable from the rest of the SELM. It was then I got my first view of the workbench.

People who work with tools for a living tend to be compulsive about them. Without the right tool, properly maintained and in good working order, a job takes significantly more time. In some cases it cannot be done at all. Learning that the hard way teaches one how to keep track of tools. I have been amazed by good mechanics who can use literally everything from their tool chest on a single repair, and never misplace anything.

Mills that do not require mechanics to supply their own tools often have an elaborate check-out system. If a tool is lost or misplaced, the cost is deducted from a worker's paycheck. Thus, by desire and design, workbenches and tool boxes tend to be well stocked and in good order. This was not the case at National.

The workbench was made from an old door, and was no larger than the average home workbench. The tools themselves were in pathetic shape. Only the remnants of a socket set existed, the open-end wrenches were incomplete, screwdrivers were broken and ground on the ends, and the Allen wrenches (by far the most impor-

In the Mill

tant tools in the shop) were kept in an old shoebox. The workbench itself was cluttered with cardboard boxes and broken parts, and Bobby had to shove some of this aside to find room to replace the broken blade. He looked through an assortment of cardboard boxes on a six-foot storage shelf on the side of the workbench to find a replacement blade. He finally found one and put it in the applicator.

He got the applicator back into the machine, but it had the same problem as before. As long as the reel of terminals was loose, it ran fine, but as soon as the slack tightened, the terminals smashed. The solution was to have me stand there and unreel the terminals by hand. I learned in the process not to unreel too many terminals at once, because the sharp edges would catch on each other and jam the machine. I also received the first of what would be an ongoing series of short but deep parallel cuts on my hands that resulted from careless handling of the terminals.

After almost two hours, Carroll rescued me and gave me another job to work on. Near the SELMs on a long table was a machine that tested the strength of terminals that had been applied. It was not working at the time, and he suggested that I take it apart and clean it. "I bet it's full of dirt and air-line lube" (a light, clear oil). Over the months I worked at National, Carroll would repeatedly see "dirt" as the cause of a problem. I soon learned to be skeptical, but now I did exactly what he told me. I took it apart, and sure enough it was full of air-line lubricant (which I got covered with), and the cylinders were dirty. I cleaned it and with some difficulty reassembled it. I reconnected it to the air line, but it behaved exactly as it had before.

By the time I had finished putting it together, the women were beginning to wash up and line up at the punch clock on the opposite side of the floor. Bobby was still at work on one of the SELMs,

Ten Hours Later

and on my way over to the sink, Carroll asked me if I wanted to "stay over" a few hours (his way of asking to work overtime). "We're way behind, and I want you to get as much knowledge as soon as you can." I stayed. I regretted it later that evening, and even more the next morning.

Ten Hours Later

It is amazing how one ten-hour-day can change your outlook. By the next morning my first day's excitement had melted into a dull, tired feeling. I was still nervous about performing the job, but it had taken only one day to dissolve my enthusiasm. There seemed to be more steps leading up to the second floor, the walls seemed drearier, and the oil from the machines more pungent. My feet were also aching from standing most of the day before.

As far as work was concerned, my second day was better than the first. Bobby got one of the SELMs running and showed me some of the simple adjustments. I learned how to change a reel of terminals and adjust the machine for various lengths of wire. To the left of the machine against a column were ten or twelve different spools of wire. They stood about three feet high and were covered by cardboard to keep the wire clean. At one point we couldn't find the color we needed, so we went down to the first floor where the wire was made.

The noise was incredible. The wire we used had a double-woven dacron insulation. On the first floor were three long rows of twenty machines, each weaving this insulation. We hung around and finally got a spool of the right wire. When we got upstairs, the SELM was not running. We knew this halfway up the stairs. Over the months at National, on my way up from the first floor or down

In the Mill

from the third, I learned to listen instinctively for the machines. After a while I was able to distinguish if one or both were running (they always ran out of phase). If they were running you breathed a sigh of relief. If they were "down" you knew someone knew exactly how long you had been gone, and you always rushed your step. When we got back on the floor, Alice, the operator of the SELM, was waving at us. It turned out that the wire had broken and needed to be rethreaded through the machine much like a film through a projector.

I hadn't seen Alice the day before because "her" machine had been down most of the day. She was a fixture at that machine when I came to the mill, and was there when I left (except for two days when she was sick). Alice was not a typical National employee. She was one of the older women and was extremely animated, always waving her hands and yelling at us across the floor. She was in her early fifties and had been with the company for four or five years. Although she earned no more than the maximum $4.25 an hour, she held one of the most important jobs on the floor. She was responsible for sorting through the completed leads (wires with terminals on the end) as they came off the machine. She rejected those that did not meet specifications and stacked those that did neatly in cardboard boxes.

It was not an easy job, and most of the women hated it. Although Alice was the steady operator on one of the SELMs, fifteen to twenty women served as operators on the other while I was at National. It was easy to see why. First was the noise. Every two seconds the terminal was applied to the wire with a crash that occurred about three feet from where the operator sat. Second, the job required speed and was very montonous. When it was running, the machine produced 3,000 leads per hour that had to be sorted. Because we were behind all the time, it was unthinkable to shut the machine down if you fell behind. However, the main reason why most women hated the SELMs was that the job demanded ongoing decision-making that had implications all the way down the line. A wrong decision would show up later down the line, and an entire assembly would have to be destroyed. It was not that the women inherently disliked making decisions, but that, as we will see, it was always necessary to make them in the midst of confusion.

The wire on Alice's SELM broke at least five times that morning, so I got plenty of practice threading it through the machine. Every time it broke, Bobby cursed the guys downstairs, and at one point got into a conversation with an older woman in her mid-forties about the wire. I remember making some kind of joke, as if she were another worker, but she responded with a sharp comeback, letting me know that she was my boss. Carroll had never introduced me to her. Later Bobby told me she was the "floor lady," June. She was in charge of the day-to-day operation of the floor and was the "straw-boss" for the women on the line. The way I met her was indicative of the confusion surrounding our relationship, and of management's style in general. It was never clear who my direct supervisior was. This created little difficulty when Carroll and June agreed, but when they didn't, I often received contradictory instructions.

Despite our awkward introduction, I quickly grew to like June. I remember thinking that in many ways she acted more like a union steward than a boss. She worked alongside the women, which helped give that impression. But more than that, she was clearly an advocate for the women. She was brassy and argued with Carroll constantly, which also helped win my respect.

But most of my second day was not spent on social relations in the mill, but trying to keep at least one of the ailing SELMs running. After a few weeks I began to list everything that could go

In the Mill

wrong with the machine. The list grew to awesome proportions. As on many multifunction machines, there were literally thousands of variables affecting the final product. As the weeks wore on, I began to wonder if the machine ever ran properly, even theoretically.

The First Day Continues

One cannot expect to learn everything about a job in two weeks. In two weeks your body is just beginning to adjust to a new routine. Yet by that time the days usually start getting easier. Some of the original fear and sense of chaos should start, to subside. This was not the case at National. Although my body was beginning to adjust to a new schedule (with lots of overtime), the high level of anxiety continued because the SELMs simply would not run correctly. As soon as we had one problem mastered, like adjusting the applicator—which took us three days—Alice would stop her machine and point out something else that was wrong. Her "yoo-hoo" became a dreaded sound.

One persistent problem at this time had to do with the stripping of the wire. Because its insulation was woven fabric, it could not be stripped by a conventional mechanical process. Instead, a unit called a "singer" (singe-er) brought two electrically heated blades together that burned a channel through the insulation. The remaining piece of insulation (which we called the slug) was then mechanically pulled off. The singer was one of the trickiest adjustments on the machine. If the heat was too low, the ends would stay on; if it were too hot, the wires would come out brown on the ends. Also, if the blades were not aligned perfectly, the strip would be uneven. We spent three days trying to get the strip right on one machine, and during the process a number of things were becoming clear.

First, it was apparent how badly the machines had been maintained. For example, when Bobby and I tried to remove the blades from the singer we discovered the adjusting screws were totally stripped. This was not the product of worker sabotage; someone simply used the wrong screwdriver, or one of many that had been ground on the end, and applied too much force. Over and over we ran into this kind of problem. A simple job would grow complicated because a bolt had been stripped or overtightened. But these were only the obvious ways in which the machines had been abused.

Because our days were spent next to, leaning on, and climbing under the SELMs, we tended to look at other parts of the machine in those few moments when it ran well. Over time you couldn't help but notice worn shafts, loose bearings, and other points of wear. One day, while waiting for the singer to cool down so that we could work on it, we took the back plate off one of the machines, exposing the internal gears and the oil reservoir. We were shocked to see that the oil was full of slugs (the stripped ends of insulation), which were circulated throughout the whole mechanism. It was at least two months before we had a chance to change it. Because we were too busy just trying to keep the machine running, all this had to wait.

It was also becoming clear that we had few spare parts. Most of the parts that cluttered the workbench and shelf belonged to other machines. Some were in other parts of the mill, others we no longer owned. Although the SELMs produced the major raw product for the floor, our accumulated spare parts fit into a cardboard container, not much bigger than a shoe box. We ran into this problem working on the singer. The blades in the machine did not match

In the Mill

up with each other, but the only other blades we had were in worse shape.

Because we had to do something and we did not have any spare parts, we did something that would make most machine mechanics cringe. Under Carroll's direction, we ground the blades on the grindstone. If there is one tool that is abused almost as much as pliers or vise grips, it is the home grindstone. A well-equipped shop actually has little need for one. But because we lacked a bench grinder or power hacksaw, we always used the grindstone when we had to cut or smooth a piece of metal. Unfortunately, a grindstone is extremely imprecise, even with the steadiest hand. It becomes worse as the piece heats up with friction. Also, a common grindstone destroys the temper (hardness) of chisels and tools with an edge, which leads to more frequent sharpenings.

Once we had ground off the legs of one of the blades for the singer we could slide it back in the assembly and adjust it properly. Carroll was proud that his solution had worked. Yet as the jaw opened and closed thousands of times in the coming weeks, it constantly went out of adjustment because we had ground off a little too much. It wasn't until we received a new blade that the problem was really solved.

When a part broke or could not be ground, a local machine shop would weld the broken part or remanufacture a new one. This is typical shop procedure, except that National used this shop in lieu of buying any spare parts. For example, we kept breaking the shear blades that Bobby broke my first day on the job. We told Carroll numerous times that we needed more blades but instead of ordering them from the company that made the machines, he had them remanufactured more cheaply in our local machine shop. The blades looked fine, but when we tried them in the SELMs, they didn't fit. I miced (measured) them with my micrometer and discovered that they were wrong on a number of dimensions. Although we tried grinding and refitting them, they never worked properly.

The lack of spare parts coupled with the general disrepair of the machines (and Bobby's very general knowledge) made it impossible to keep the SELMs running for any length of time. As two weeks turned into a month this situation became maddening. It was like a month of first days on the job. We were so tied to the SELMs that I had little time to learn about the mill or the rest of my job. Furthermore, we could set no priorities in repair. Rather than do a major repair, which we did not have time for, we often jerry-rigged or "Mickey-Moused" it, as Bobby would say.

In addition, all our repair work was performed at a frantic pace. The SELMs produced the basic material for the shop floor, and our limping machines could hardly produce enough. Moreover, instead of running one of the six colors of wire that the machine produced for an extended period of time, we were constantly changing from one color to another. Because each set up took at least a half an hour, we continued to lose production time.

So when the machines were not running, or running well, it was no trival matter. It was not as though production could be shifted to another area. Each time a machine was down, as the minutes ticked away, first June and then Carroll would hover around offering advice, which only increased the pressure. Situations like this, when you find yourself working in a fishbowl, only add to the tension.

During one of these moments, I was setting up the machine for a color change when my wrench slipped and fell onto the cover of the machine with a bang. This sort of thing happens even among highly experienced mechanics. Yet as I turned to retrieve the wrench, I saw Carroll watching me. I will never forget his incrim-

In the Mill

inating look. I was finally beginning to understand Bobby's demeanor and how it was so much an outgrowth of these kinds of situations.

Jerry-rigged equipment, repaired under conditions of frenzy, had other effects besides lowering productivity. During my employment I witnessed two serious injuries, both of which are not typical of light assembly work. One expects minor burns from soldering, cuts and abrasions from handling sharp terminals and working around sewing machine needles, and as in any manufacturing facility, an occasional accident. The events I witnessed fit none of these categories.

The first accident occurred late one afternoon while we were rushing to get an order out by the end of the day. Carroll was on the floor, as he often was at such times, hurrying the "girls" along. He hovered over one of the newer sewers, and I saw him looking at his watch from time to time. Under this pressure she somehow placed her finger in the path of the machine (which was not easy to do) and ran the needle solidly into her finger. It is not the seriousness of this accident that is significant, but the manner in which it occurred. Safe conditions are difficult to achieve under these direct kinds of pressure.

The second accident resulted less from supervisory pressure than from faulty equipment. On the third floor National manufactured coupling cables for computers. Most people probably imagine that high-tech manufacturing uses high-tech methods, but our operation was quite different. For example, we used an ordinary paper cutter to cut our one-inch multiconductor computer cable to length. It was patently the wrong tool for the job. Anyone who has used paper cutters knows that they can be dangerous. A worker who had been at National less than a month lost the end of his thumb to this paper cutter.

Machinery and Chaos in Production

I suspect that many small shops have unsafe conditions similar to those at National. Jerry-rigged and inappropriate equipment under conditions of confusion combine to create less than safe workplaces. As well, many small shops are less subject to regular on-site inspections by OSHA than larger facilities.[1] For example, we had a recurring problem with fumes from a dangerous industrial solvent, MEK (Methyl Ethyl Ketone).[2] We used it to clean parts in machine repair and to clean cables and connectors prior to soldering. Its use would probably have been more closely monitored at a larger plant, but the problem persisted at National despite our complaints.

Machinery and Chaos in Production

It should be clear just how poorly the machinery at National ran. Sometimes machines stopped through sheer lack of oil. Often they produced in a day what they should have produced in an hour.

The machinery had three major problems. First, most of it was outdated for the kind of operation we were running, and it had been badly maintained over the years. Second, management refused to stock either enough spare parts or the tools necessary to repair machines.

Third, management refused to hire or keep trained personnel to maintain the machines. Instead, they hired a series of young inexperienced mechanics (some better, some worse) who, if they were

1. It should be noted that under the Reagan administration on-site inspections have been severely reduced. See, for example, the AFL-CIO Report, *Workers in Jeopardy: OSHA Under the Reagan Administration* (September 1984).

2. On the hazards of MEK, see Nick H. Proctor and James P. Hughes, *Chemical Hazards of the Workplace* (Philadelphia: J. B. Lippincott, 1978).

In the Mill

lucky, managed to keep the deteriorating equipment patched together.[3]

These three factors combined to create a vicious circle that was difficult to break. Because we had improper tools, screws were stripped. Because screws were stripped, even simple repairs became difficult. Ill-fitting parts often caused as many problems as they solved. Because we were inexperienced, we often attacked symptoms instead of the problem itself. This wasted our time, which could have been used for preventive maintenance. I often discovered that a problem with a machine had been created by someone who disassembled it and put it back together improperly. In this way, in terms of basic equipment and machinery, we can see that National varies from the conventional view of the rational industrial workplace. Already the waste built into the production system is apparent.

Although this level of decrepit and ill-maintained machinery is probably more characteristic of small shops, larger firms are not immune. Indeed, a general criticism of American industry is its failure to modernize. A prime example is the steel industry.[4] We are presently trying to compete with the Japanese, but with machinery that was state-of-the-art in the 1940s and 1950s. Although I would not suggest that the entire steel industry operates machinery as de-

3. Although I had no access to personnel records, from what I could ascertain there had been six or seven mechanics over the past three years. With the exception of one man in his mid-thirties, the rest of the mechanics were in their early twenties and stayed on the average less than six months.

4. For a discussion of the failure of the steel industry to reinvest in new equipment and its effect on the industry, see Staughton Lynd, *The Fight Against Shutdowns: Youngstown's Steelmill Closings* (San Pedro, Calif.: Miles and Weir, 1982).

crepit as National's, I suspect that many of the same tendencies exist as old, outdated equipment is pushed to compete.

Furthermore, conditions like these at National often result when a large multinational corporation buys out a small manufacturing firm in search of quick profit. For example, after the Morse Twist Drill Company was purchased by Gulf and Western, it spent only 10 per cent, between 1977 and 1980, of what two Morse competitors invested in new machinery and maintenance (Harrison, 1982). Additionally, the company cut maintenance and machine training for employees (Harrison, 1982a).[5] As this kind of disinvestment continues (Bluestone and Harrison, 1982), a growing number of American workers will find themselves working with outdated, ill-repaired machinery.

The inadequate machinery and the sporadic production at National sets the stage for much of the other activity that occurred on the shop floor. As we will see, the problems that resulted from the short-term decisions of management pervaded the social relations of production as well.

5. For more on the Morse Twist Drill disinvestment, see the entire issue of *Labor Research Review* 1 (Fall 1982).

3. Women on the Line

Until recently, the role played by women in the industrial labor force has been severely underestimated. Although the postwar bias emphasized the extent to which women remained in the home, women have played fundamental roles in American industry; as Barbara Wertheimer has written, "We Were There" (Wertheimer, 1977). We tend to forget that it was women who first left the New England farms (leaving the men behind) to work in the new industrial centers of Lawrence, Massachusetts and Manchester, New Hampshire.[1] In addition, entire industries, such as the garment industry, hired primarily female workers.

It is important, however, to characterize the nature of women's participation in the industrial labor force. Despite great shifts in American industry (textiles in New England have been replaced by high-tech, for example), "women's work" has remained essentially the same.[2] For the most part women have occupied the lowest paid, most tedious "handwork" positions. In the textile industry women

1. For general treatments of Lawrence and Manchester, see William Cahn, *Lawrence 1912* (New York: The Pilgrim Press, 1980); and Tamara K. Hareven and Randolph Langerbach, *Amoskeag: Life and Work in the American Factory-City* (New York: Pantheon, 1980).

2. For more on the rise of the high-tech industry in New England see Bennett Harrison, *The Economic Transformation of New England since World War II* (Cambridge, Mass.: Joint Center for Urban Studies of MIT and Harvard University, 1982); and Sarah Kuhn, *Computer Manufacturing in New England* (Cambridge, Mass.: Joint Center for Urban Studies of MIT and Harvard University, 1982).

Women on the Line

nimbly replaced spools of thread and tied swift weavers' knots as well as similar handwork.[3] In today's high-tech industry they assemble electrical components and micro chips. As in the garment industry, women hold the majority of assembly positions (Grossman, 1980).

Thus the women at National are part of a continuing American tradition, one that our conventional view of the industrial workplace has generally downplayed. In what follows we will observe assembly work at National—and see that in addition to low pay and repetition, it is characterized by a considerable degree of chaos.

Women's Work

On the average there were twenty women working on the second floor at National. The number fluctuated greatly while I was there. It plummeted to a low of eight during two different lay-offs, and rose to forty during peak production (for about two months when a four-hour second shift was added). The women were extremely young. A handful were in their forties and fifties, but most were in their early twenties. At least eight were under twenty.

There were ten to fifteen small machines on the floor that were used sporadically for a variety of jobs. Two or three might be running at any given time. But most of the women worked on the three-wire assembly, the major product of the floor. The production of these assemblies was broken down into six separate tasks.

The process began at the SELM, where terminals were placed on

3. For more on the nature of women's work in textile mills see Hareven and Langerbach, *Amoskeag.*

various lengths of wire. It was the operator's job to inspect these leads (wires) as they came off the machine. They were then stacked in cardboard boxes and put in a shelf near the SELM at the back of the floor.

The assembly itself began in the next phase. Between four and eight women took three different colors (and lengths) of wire and inserted them into a small plastic block an inch square and a quarter of an inch deep. This was by far the hardest and most tedious job. Each lead had a square terminal on the end which had to be pushed into a square channel in the plastic block until it locked. It was not an easy task. It took a certain amount of force and some finesse as well. If you held the lead too far back you bent the terminal. If you held the lead too close you banged your fingers.

You could always tell who was new on the job by their bandaged fingers. Without exception, new employees were assigned to "blocking," as this job was called, and without exception their hands bled. If they lasted beyond the first few weeks, which most did not, they developed the calluses neccessary to do the job.

Besides being physically difficult, "blocking" demanded speed. The women were expected to block close to two hundred assemblies per hour, although we had no bonus system (where workers can earn extra money by being more productive). If after a training period that rate was not met, the women would be called into the office repeatedly and threatened with dismissal, although to my knowledge that never happened. Usually they quit long before that.

From the blockers the assemblies moved down the line to be sewed. Although I use the phrase "down the line," the assemblies were not moved down a belt or automatic assembly line. They were stacked in boxes which the women shifted from station to station.

Women on the Line

At any given time the floor was stacked with a variety of boxes containing assemblies at different stages of production. The sewers took assemblies that had been blocked and on specially designed machines sewed around the three wires. Sewing was the most favored job on the line, and it was usually assigned to women who had been at National the longest. The younger women competed hard for these positions.

The assemblies then passed to the singers (singe-ers) and trimmers. The actual stitching of the assemblies was fairly loose, and it was the singer's job to pass a heat gun (which looked like a large hair dryer) over the stitching to shrink the thread around the wires. After singeing, the loose end of the thread was cut off by the trimmers. In many ways the easiest job, trimming, was often held back as a reward or to be done when there was little else to do.

These five steps—making the leads on the SELM, blocking, sewing, singeing, and trimming—produced the assembly. The sixth and final stage was to inspect and pack the finished product. The inspectors checked the length of the wire, the sewing, the blocks (to see that they were not scratched in the blocking process), and a variety of other characteristics. Depending on the work load, one or two women worked as inspectors.

For a while my knowledge of the women's work was only that of an outsider. I had observed them repeating their tasks over and over, but my attention had been focused on the SELMs. Their work seemed straightforward, and although boring, appeared to present little confusion. Yet in the coming months, as I spent more time with the women, I began to understand that their work was quite different. Although these six tasks appeared so simple that one would expect the process to be automatic, it was actually the source of much confusion, conflict, and disagreement. A careful look at the production process reveals why women on the line were beset with their own kind of chaos.

The Craft Knowledge of Deskilled Workers

Much has been written about the deskilling of labor in the twentieth century. Perhaps the best example is Harry Braverman's *Labor and Monopoly Capital* (1974). Throughout the book, as well as in related volumes (see Zimbalist, 1979), we are given numerous examples of how technology has taken away the skill from a job, leaving only routine to the workers.

If there ever were an example of this degradation of labor, it was the kind of work performed by the women at National. There is no way that their work could be seen as exciting, satisfying, or rewarding. It was tolerable at best. Even Carroll recognized this. He once told me, "It takes a special kind of girl [sic] to do this kind of work. The guys could never do it, they don't have the patience. We like the neat ones, the ones who like this close work."

One comes away from Braveman convinced that little skill is necessary to perform most factory jobs. This conviction is very much shared as a conventional wisdom. Yet these "simple" tasks often look quite different from the shop floor.

One of my first jobs working closely with the women involved changing the belts on the sewing machines. The belts were made of leather and stretched or broke over time. Installing a new belt involved cutting a new piece of leather to the proper length and fastening it together with a metal staple. This took about half an hour (until much later when I discovered a special tool which was designed to punch the holes and fasten the staple). The women poked

Women on the Line

fun at my somewhat clumsy style (the task actually was quite difficult), especially Carol (not to be confused with Carroll), whose machine I started on. She was a large woman in her late thirties with a hot temper but also a good sense of humor.

After replacing the belt, I sat down at her machine and asked her to show me how to sew. I never heard such laughter. The other women thought that a man sewing was the funniest thing they ever saw. It took me five minutes to sew a single assembly, and it came out completely wrong. "You'll never make your rate that way, honey," said Carol. "You think your job is hard," said one of the other sewers. Carroll would also sew while repairing or testing a machine. He was a little better at it than me, but not much. The women used the opportunity to give him all the grief they could. "See if you can keep that up all day," one of the women used to say.

It was clear to me, and to anyone else watching, that a worker could not walk in off the street, sit down at the machine, and make her rate. Yet despite his own experience, this is how Carroll often threatened the women: "Why, I could get somebody right off the street who could do that job faster than you." Perhaps Carroll believed it. The usual explanation is that these jobs require a certain manual dexterity, though no real skill, and some people simply lack the physical coordination. Yet this explanation is not adequate. As I found out, many of our assembly positions required more than deftness.

At one point I was called over to adjust a small press. It applied a spade terminal (like the one on your television antenna) to an already cut and stripped length of wire. The repair amounted essentially to cleaning out the applicator with the air line and some lubricant, but in the process I discovered that Betty, the operator of the machine, had perfected an ingenious technique.

The Craft Knowledge of Deskilled Workers

The wire was approximately sixteen inches long, and terminals had to be placed on each end parallel to each other. I had seen other women struggle with this job, placing a terminal on one end, turning the wire around, lining it up and applying the other terminal. Betty, however, had found another way to do it. As I was checking the machine, I saw her pick up a handful of wires and bounce them in her hand. When I asked what she was doing, she said she was finding the "bend" in the wire. This 'bend' she referred to was due to the fact that the wire had originally been coiled on a spool. Although the machine that stripped and cut the wire included a mechanical device called a straightener, it was impossible to remove the bend entirely, and when lined up in a tray, the wires bent one way or the other.

Once Betty had bounced the wires and they lined up the same way (with the ends bending down as she held them); still holding them as a bunch, she put a terminal on one end of all of them. She then turned the bundle around and put terminals on the other end. Because she let the memory of the wire keep the ends turned the same way, the terminals were easily applied in the proper parallel fashion.

I was impressed. This was hardly a deskilled worker performing routine procedures. When I asked her how she learned to do it, she responded casually that she had figured it out doing the job. As I began to see the women's work from the inside, I noticed a host of skills like Betty's that facilitated production. In fact, I was surprised how fundamental this "craft knowledge" was to the day-to-day operation of the mill. By "craft knowledge," most people think of skills posessed by someone like a violin maker. It is knowledge that cannot be rigidly systematized or reduced to procedural rules but is developed through years of experience. I would argue that

51

Women on the Line

the women on the line possessed skills very much akin to those of a craftsman.

Even so, I would hardly argue that working in National was anything like making violins. Indeed, as we have seen, the work itself was menial. Yet contrary to Braverman, a job that involves repetitive, boring tasks is not necessarily devoid of skill or craft. As Manwaring and Wood conclude, the recognition of "working knowledge does not in and of itself refute the deskilling thesis, but it does provide a different vantage point, one in which the central notion is that work is both degrading and constructive, both crippling and enriching" (Manwaring and Wood, 1984: 56).

It is not that craft knowledge at National merely facilitated speedier production. Rather, it was integral to getting the job done at all. Based on research in a paper cone factory, Ken Kusterer (1978) implies this point in his distinction between basic and supplemental (craft) knowledge.

> Basic knowledge includes all the procedures necessary to routinely carry out their work tasks: how to start and stop the machine, clean it in a prescribed manner, "bridge the cones", label the case, etc. Supplemental knowledge includes all the know-how necessary to handle obstacles to this routine work performance that arise from time to time: how to keep the machinery running, overcome "bad paper," diagnose the cause of the defects (Kusterer, 1978: 45).

Thus, when Carroll told the women that he could replace them with "somebody off the street," what he really meant was, "Provided that all the materials are perfect, the machines are running well, and with constant supervision," then "somebody off the street" would do. But as we have seen, National hardly ever ran under those conditions. The machines were in constant disrepair, the materials were inconsistent, and most of the actual decisions on the floor were made by the women themselves, not by Carroll or June. If the managers had to make every decision themselves, production schedules would never be met.

The high labor turnover at National always threatened production. A new assembler would be trained for a day or two and then left on her own. This worked fine as long as things went smoothly. But a problem could spell disaster. For example, one new blocker was doing fine until she blocked 5,000 assemblies with wire that was too heavy. A more experienced blocker would have detected the overly heavy gauge simply by feeling the wire, and could have avoided the lost time and materials. (In a way Carroll was right about taking workers directly off the street. This blocker had made her rate all right, but her work had to be tossed in the scrap pile.)

Thus, the day-to-day operation of the mill required more than mere routine assembly. Yet the constant need for decision-making had mixed implications for the women on the line.

Chaos on the Line

As Kusterer demonstrates in *Know-How on the Job* (1978), all jobs from bank teller to longshoreman demand an insider's knowledge, without which the job cannot be done effectively. This craft knowledge is important to workers in a number of ways. First, it is an important source of pride and dignity. That jobs involve more than menial tasks contributes in fundamental ways to workers' self-esteem.[4] Second, craft knowledge can be an important source

4. See Tony Manwaring and Stephen Wood. "The Ghost in the Machine: Tacit Skills in the Labor Process," *Socialist Review* 74 (March–April 1984): 77–79.

of power for workers. Because for the most part it is hidden from management, it can become a tool for workers to assert power in the workplace.

Yet the degree to which this kind of decision-making was constantly needed on the line indicates how confused production really was. The women did not really mind making decisions—it was by far the most interesting part of their day—but making the right decision was not always clear, and the wrong decision often carried strong sanctions.

For example, the leads produced by the SELM were supposed to be measured on an ongoing basis by the operator and once an hour by an inspector. They checked the overall length of the wire, the length of the strip, and how the wire was placed in the terminal. The specifications for these leads were extremely rigid, with the tolerance on each measure plus or minus one-sixty-fourth of an inch. Given the condition of the machines, the quality of the materials, and the experience of the workers, this tolerance was nearly impossible to achieve. In fact, the manual for the machine specified that it would work only to a one-thirty-second of an inch tolerance. In actuality, the machines were running plus or minus one-sixteenth of an inch.

Everyone in the mill, from the operator Alice to the inspectors, was aware of this. They knew that by official specifications most of the leads were beyond tolerance. Yet they also knew that the leads were probably acceptable to the purchaser, and that if they rejected too many items Carroll would be on their backs. Thus everyone was in an ambiguous position that required a constant negotiation of the rules.

From my experience, this goes on in other mills, where official specifications only serve as general guidelines, and where actual specifications are actually much looser. Yet I never witnessed anywhere near the negotiation that occurred daily at National. If the women actually obeyed the specifications, they would do no work. Yet if they accepted (or produced) something beyond an acceptable tolerance, they ran the risk of being held responsible for producing "bad" items.

This uncertainty led to endless "crises" at National. Every two or three weeks, management shut down the production line and called everyone into the cafeteria. Carroll or June would show us some assemblies and ask us what was wrong with them. It was a test. It was amazing how much we could find wrong if we looked hard enough, although what we found was often not what they had in mind. One time the blocks were scratched, another time the tab on the end of the terminals was bent, and once the sewing pulled out. They would chew us out and send us back to the line, usually with some new procedure or inspection to eliminate the problem.

However, if we focused on one detail or aspect of production, the line would immediately slow down. As long as the women stuck close to specifications, the production rate dropped. Interestingly, most of these crises ended the same way. For a week or two the women were very careful, but before long they went back to their old ways. The new inspection or procedure was usually forgotten, and the uncertainty in the production line remained essentially the same. It was amazing to me that despite a series of these crises, the line ran basically the same when I left National as when I arrived.

Much More Than Just a Routine Job

From this in-depth look at the women on the line at National, we have discovered that what they do is much more than just routine work. Not denying that it was boring and repetitive, working at National required constant decision-making and precarious negotiation of what was expected. At first glance, it might be argued

Women on the Line

that the women at National were "lucky" to have this high level of decision-making, to the extent that it relieved them of the boredom they would otherwise experience. Yet upon further analysis, this constant decision-making cannot be seen as relieving boredom. Decision-making took place in such a confusing and contradictory context that in fundamental ways it added to the pressure.

Workers have a number of ways of dealing with monotony. For some it is dreams of summer vacations or a new car, for others it is the beer at lunch, while others try radios and singing on the job. If you observe a mill carefully, you will notice all kinds of routines that appear pointless at first glance. For example, one of the older women on the floor had a routine she followed religiously. Every day at morning coffeebreak she went to the corner store and bought a newspaper. She brought it to her table and then went to the bathroom for a paper towel that she spread on her table. She then proceeded to eat half of her sandwich, no more, no less, every working day. There were numerous other examples of women "setting up" their meager possessions—radio, cigarettes, and coffee cup—in similar fashion.

At first you wonder if these routines are the product of working too long in an alienating workplace. Yet over time you see the purpose behind these rituals. Most of what the workers at National did was out of their control. They knew they would produce thousands of assemblies each day, yet had no control over the conditions under which that production occurred. These rituals, then, in important and fundamental ways served to impose some, if only a small amount, of personal impact on the day. The woman who eats just half a sandwich at the same time each day in her own way is imposing some order on the day's events. Although these jobs are clearly "too small for people," it is through this imposition of order that they somehow become "enough."

Much More Than Just a Routine Job

Jobs become less boring to the extent that workers control their daily activities. For example, if workers' rates were computed by the day instead of by the hour, workers could work harder in the morning when they were fresh, and slower in the afternoon when tired. A break in the work routine, however, when not tied to an increase in control, does not necessarily make a job less boring. For instance, when management stopped production at National because of problems with tolerances, it did not alleviate boredom. Since constant decision-making made the workday more unpredictable, the women felt less in control than if their jobs were utterly routine.

Psychologists agree that random punishment is the worst kind because it threatens an individual's sense of control and order.[5] A punishment that follows from a certain behavior or occurs at some fixed interval is much easier to deal with than one that occurs at random times. In a similar fashion, the ongoing decision-making and the confusion that resulted made the work at National difficult to bear.

Especially confusing times (during one of our "crises," for instance) had an obvious effect on the women who worked on the line. Tempers flared, arguments were more common, people took more days off, and some worked as slowly as they could. They complained as well. "I wish they'd make up their damn minds," said one of the blockers to me. "It's bad enough having such boring work, and then there's so much confusion all the time. One day it'll pass, the next day it won't." As another woman said to me, "All I want to do is to be able to do my job without anyone bothering me, and then go home."

5. For example, see B. F. Skinner, *Contingencies of Reinforcement* (New York: Appleton-Century-Crofts, 1969).

4. Management and the Continuation of Chaos

W E HAVE SEEN HOW, WHEN VIEWED
from the shop floor, production at National turned out to be quite
disorganized and confused. Some of the disorganization resulted
from National's size and its inability to formalize and routinize
many of its operations. Yet, it should be apparent that much of the
confusion resulted from management decisions (and indecisions).
In this chapter I will focus on this connection between management and the continuation of chaos.

Due to a number of factors, but chiefly the influence of an outside engineer, we had a excellent chance to improve the conditions
of the machinery at National, thereby reducing some of the shop-
floor confusion. Despite the tendency toward ad hoc production,
these improvements could have greatly improved productivity
(and subsequently profit) as well as working conditions. The way
in which management failed to realize this potential proved reveal-
ing. It demonstrated the flaws in making decisions based on short-
term economic considerations. Indeed, *short-term* myopia created
much of the *long-term* confusion on the shop floor.

However, shortsighted decisions do not explain all the irrationality at National. A management style that stressed centralized control was also to blame. Indeed, management refused to allow
workers to participate in decision-making and insisted on complete control even if it meant a loss of productivity and profit.

Such rigidity comes at great cost; it "not only dampened productive investment and reduced capacity utilization, but it also
moderated pressure on corporations to sustain the pace of productive innovation" (Bowles, Gordon, and Weisskopf, 1983: 135). At

Management and the Continuation of Chaos

National, this attitude helped perpetuate the cycle of irrationality on the shop floor.

Getting the Machines Running

Despite my earlier doubts, we were able to get the SELMs running with surprising regularity by my fourth month. They were far from perfect, but for the first time both machines ran over half the time. This improvement stemmed from a number of factors.

The first was time. Despite the decrepit state of the machines and our limited knowledge, four months of constant attention was beginning to show. Like the women on the line, we were developing our own craft knowledge. Some problems occurred over and over again, and we began to develop solutions (if only jerry-rigged ones). Additionally, we were beginning to understand the parameters of our work and the limitations we had to work within. For example, if one machine was down we learned to keep the other running at all costs, so as not to fall too far behind.

Perhaps most important was learning how problems were related to one another. Because the SELMs performed so many functions, it was not always clear where the problem lay, and it was not enough to understand each function independently of the others. For example, when a terminal was being applied incorrectly, it was often difficult to tell whether the problem lay in the conveyor that delivered the wire to the applicator, or in the applicator itself. To make matters more complex, the two systems were "bridged" (interfaced) by a part called the wire positioner, which although a part of neither system, positioned the wire prior to the terminal being applied. A successful application required all three of these elements, both independently and in conjunction, to work correctly. Over time we were beginning to understand interactions like this.

Getting the Machines Running

Time alone, however, would not have led to higher production on the SELMs. Although our knowledge was increasing in some areas, there were others in which we were totally lost. For example, the electrical relay system that hung beneath the machine in an enclosed box was a complete mystery, and nothing short of instruction from an experienced electrician would have allowed us to understand it. Self-exploration in some areas was not enough. What pushed us over this threshold was the arrival of Pete Kraft, an engineer from the company that manufactured the SELMs.

Although the machines were finally running better we had encountered a recurrent and aggravating problem. From time to time the applicator would bend the end of the terminal, which hindered blocking and increased the likelihood of scratching the blocks. We were struggling with this problem when Carroll finally decided to call for outside help. "This is costing us $150.00 a day, so see that you both pay attention." Looking at me, he said, "Make sure you take notes and we'll post them on the side of the machine."

When the engineer from ABC (the company that made SELMs) arrived, it was like the entrance of a knight in shining armor. Bobby and I always wore our oldest clothes because we got dirty regularly and the company refused to make arrangements for uniforms (even at our own expense).[1] Pete Kraft, however, always

---

1. The issue of uniforms is a microcosm of National. Working around machines can be extremely dirty, and in most industrial mills mechanics rent industrial uniforms. A number of us wanted this arrangement at National, and offered to pay for our own uniforms if the company would have them delivered (it is nearly impossible to rent a uniform directly from the supplier). After a series of postponements the company refused to make the arrangements. They felt it would create too much confusion in the shop, and that they would have to supply lockers. Thus we were left in our oldest, dirtiest clothes. When Pete walked in dressed in a suit, the consequences became clear. In a uniform you are a professional, a bona fide mechanic. In your old clothes, you are just a hack, an amateur.

Management and the Continuation of Chaos

came to work in a suit and tie, and often in a light-colored suit. He also carried a briefcase, but instead of holding papers it contained the most complete and excellent set of tools I had ever seen. Bobby and I would talk about those tools for hours after Pete left, and we dreamed about having tools that fine.

Company representatives like Pete Kraft serve a number of roles. First of all, they perform public relations for their own company. It was interesting to see how hard Pete worked to treat everyone at National with respect. Although he grew to dislike Carroll, he concealed it from him. In addition, company representatives act as salesmen, urging companies to upgrade and add to their equipment.

We had representatives from other companies visit the shop. Most of them were strong on public relations and sales, but weak on repairs. One representative called in to fix a high-speed stripping and cutting machine actually never made repairs at all, but spent the better part of a day demonstrating a new computerized $26,000 machine.

Pete was good at public relations and sales (he soon learned that National would probably never upgrade its equipment), but he was also an excellent nuts-and-bolts mechanic. He did not fit the stereotype most mechanics have of engineers (that is, someone who knows how things work theoretically, but cannot deal with the practicalities of running a machine in a factory setting). He could read an electrical schematic and use a voltmeter (neither Bobby nor I could), but he also had a sharp eye and keen trouble-shooting mind.

On his first visit to the shop he took an applicator from one of the machines and went through it piece by piece. He commented on how dirty the parts were, and gave us guidelines for cleaning and greasing them. This introduction to the applicator took about two hours. After we put the applicator back into the machine he showed us how to adjust it so it would apply the terminal correctly (the problem Bobby struggled with my first day in the mill). It took him less than five minutes, and I finally understood why we had such difficulty. We had seen two adjustments as a coarse and fine adjustment of a single adjustment, when in fact, as Pete showed us, they adjusted two separate parts.

For the rest of the afternoon Bobby and I took turns putting the applicator out of adjustment and then resetting it. When the buzzer rang for wash-up we were still slower than Pete, but we felt proud of ourselves. To think of all the time we had spent trying every conceivable adjustment, yet never really understanding how the adjustments worked.

We learned a number of other things during Pete's first visit, although not specifically about machine repair. To our surprise, he told us that National did not own the SELMs, but leased them from ABC. Not only were they leased, but the ABC company was responsible for maintaining them. This meant that except for the applicators, ABC was also responsible for all parts. Parts did not cost National anything—nor did Pete charge the $150.00 a day that Carroll had told us. He charged only for repairs caused by negligence.

Carroll shrugged all this off, as if he knew it already. But if he did, why hadn't he called Pete in earlier? If the machines were covered by some kind of service contract, there was no excuse for their miserable condition. Pete also mentioned that we could attend a special school (at no charge) to learn about the machines, if the company approved. When we approached Carroll, he shrugged that off too. "Oh, we've done that before, but as soon as we do, the guys come back thinking they know everything and then they leave." And that was the end of that subject.

Management and the Continuation of Chaos

Keeping the Machines Running

During the next month Pete came in regularly and showed us more about the machines. We also started tackling some of the major problems. Unlike Carroll, who was often agitated by mechanical difficulties, Pete seemed fascinated by them. I think he liked coming to National partly because our machines presented him with a challenge. I have described how poorly the SELMs worked. Pete had travelled to hundreds of shops in the Northeast, and he confirmed my judgment: "These babies are running on borrowed time," he would say.[2]

Pete explained that the machines leased to National were an early product of his company. They were actually the hybrid of two machines—one built by another company that cut and stripped wire had been attached to an ABC machine that applied terminals. ABC had given up on this design some years ago, and their new models performed all the functions in a much simpler fashion.

To Pete's knowledge, we were one of few companies using this older machine at all, let alone on an ongoing basis. One of the SELMs was so old that it no longer appeared on the company's records. Although ABC continued service, National essentially paid no rent on it. Pete often commented how surprised he was that we based our whole production line on these machines.

One of the first big problems we tackled together was with one of the machines that was not supplying a terminal to every tenth

2. Later I asked Pete how National compared to other shops he visited. He said that although most were better, National was not the worst. He generally confirmed our thesis that the small, semiautonomous shops were the poorest and that the larger companies were generally in better shape. That some shops were worse than National, confirmed my belief that National is typical of a certain kind of production facility.

wire or so that came down the conveyor. While working on this problem we got our first lesson on one of the black boxes (the "press," as it was called) whose mechanism baffled us. Sitting on top of the machine, the press consisted of a fifty-pound flywheel driven by a motor, and a mechanism which when triggered applied the force of the flywheel down to the applicator (which then applied the terminal). There seemed to be some problem in the mechanism that released the flywheel. The mechanism was located behind the flywheel, so the flywheel had to come off.

We had to hammer the flywheel off with a ten-pound hammer and a two-by-four. Only then did we realize what a mess it was. The press had two grease fittings, and although we had never greased them while I had been at National, at some point someone had "greased the hell out of it," as Pete said. The mechanism was covered with grease, which for many machines would be no serious problem. However, in this specific mechanism the power was transferred from the flywheel by a series of thirteen nylon rollers. It was in fact the friction between these rollers and the flywheel that caused the applicator to "depress." Because it was so filled with grease (a lubricant) it was no wonder that it was not working properly.

We spent the better part of the afternoon cleaning the assembly and getting it back together. While we were cleaning it, Pete asked how often we oiled and greased the machines. He shook his head when we told him only occasionally, and we decided that the machines should be oiled daily and greased once a week. "It would be a different thing if you were only running these things a few hours a day, but because you're running the hell out of them, you'd better keep them well oiled," Pete concluded.

Some of the abuse these machines suffered was easy to identify, but often it was hidden and subtle. This turned out to be the case with the "press" we thought we had just fixed. Although we thought we had solved the problem by a simple clean-up, it began recurring again.

At first the problem was only intermittent, but it rapidly became as bad as before. Pete came back and we tried to figure out what was wrong. We watched the machine in operation, listened, and waited for it to skip. Pete was much more patient than Bobby and I. I was unsure what we were listening for. After a while, Pete pointed out that every time the machine failed to apply a terminal, the solenoid in the unit buzzed. (A solenoid is a device that takes an electrical impulse and through an electromagnet converts it into a mechanical motion.) Once a wire was in place it triggered a switch that "energized" the solenoid. The movement of the solenoid triggered the mechanism that released the flywheel.

Pete commented that the solenoid was a trouble spot on these machines, so we replaced it and reassembled the mechanism. This time it was my turn to lift the fifty-pound flywheel to chest height and slide it carefully onto a finely turned shaft. Pete left assured that we had solved the problem once and for all.

Yet like a bad dream the problem started coming back. It would start and stop, but finally it reached a point where we were producing too much scrap to keep the machine running. Once again we pulled the flywheel (this time without Pete's assistance) and after a lot of head scratching and searching discovered that one of the parts of the mechanism was broken. In fact, it might have been broken all the time.

We called Pete with the part number, but because our machines were so old, it was out of stock and would take ten days to be custom made. We ordered it, but in the meantime had the broken part welded so we could get the machine running. When the problem resurfaced yet once more, we pulled the flywheel and discovered that the same part had broken again, not on the weld, but next to it. It did not make sense. If the mechanism was working properly, then no more than finger pressure would have been applied to it. Obviously, something else was wrong.

We finally discovered the real cause. At the point where two parts that activated the mechanism met, years of constant use had created a ridge on what was supposed to be a smooth surface. The machine sometimes skipped when the moving part stuck on this ridge. This prevented the solenoid from doing its job, causing it to buzz, and also put undue pressure on the part that broke. We smoothed out the ridge with a file and emory cloth and kept it well greased. It never caused us any trouble again.

This instance exemplifies the nature of machine repair. I followed Carroll's directive and took as many notes as I could, but I often found them worthless afterwards. For example, what should I have written down about the problem with the press? The service manual listed all the parts and how they were assembled. The rest of what I learned was not easily reducible to some set of rules or directives that could, as Carroll suggested, be posted on the side of the machine. Even for Pete, who was an extremely experienced mechanic, this repair was more trial and error and less "technically formal" than we might imagine.

The nature of machine repair seems quite different from Carroll's "theory" of what it ought to be. Only to a small degree did Pete provide us with information that could be written down and used again. Our knowledge was more craft-like than Carroll's more mechanistic view suggested. As we will see, the fact that machine repair depended on intuition and craft became a source of difficulty in the coming months. The reason was obvious: the less that machine repair was reducible to public rules and procedures, the less it fell under Carroll's direct control.

A New Kind of Pride

Having machines that ran regularly was not the only effect of Pete's visits to National. Both Bobby and I were able to take new pride in our work. This was true even when the machines did not run. Instead of muddled guesswork, we now had some idea at least where to start. If not, we knew we could call Pete, and that he would stop by in two or three days.

The nature of repair work made it impossible to fully routinize our activities. Yet our new-found knowledge allowed us to impose considerably more control on the day's events. For example, at Pete's suggestion we instituted a maintenance log where we recorded each time we oiled and greased a machine, or any other repair. As we had agreed, each morning Bobby and I oiled the SELMs, took out the applicators, cleaned and greased them. It took about fifteen minutes (unless you discovered a problem, which was one reason to institute the procedure).

Although this change might appear minor in the course of a day's events, for us it was not. It was always hard to start a repair or jump into the confusion first thing in the morning. Bobby used to say, "I'm too hung over to get near that press." The oiling gave us a routine. It happened each and every day no matter what, and it eased our entry into the day.

The instituting of a daily oiling had other consequences. For the first time, the start-up of the machines did not depend on Carroll or June or the buzzer, but on Bobby and me. We exerted control not only over the beginning of our own work day, but on that of others. This may seem like a meager form of control, but it was significant to us and it led to an increase in pride.

It is difficult to regard the changes that resulted from Pete's visits as anything but beneficial. The machines were running hundreds of per cent better, and at times we actually surpassed the women's demand for leads. We were on the road to regular maintenance, and we were correcting problems that had developed over years of neglect. Bobby and I felt better and performed our jobs more competently. (It is noteworthy that we began cleaning up our work area and the floor in general for the first time. I also mustered the courage to ask for my first raise.) Yet this new sense of pride also proved a new source of chaos.

A New Kind of Chaos

Although Carroll was pleased with the changes on the floor, especially with the increased production, he seemed disquieted at the same time. Perhaps it is more accurate to say that he was ambivalent. He rather sheepishly explained that although he had pushed hard for my raise, it was turned down upstairs because the company was having a bad quarter. This seemed to indicate mixed feelings about how he and his superiors felt about our work.

His ambivalence was also reflected in his attitude to us. He was almost always pleased with the end result of our work, but he did not always approve of how we went about it. For example, while we were trying to solve the problem of the press that skipped leads, Carroll saw us standing around the machine. "What are you guys doing?" he asked. Taking a lesson from Pete, we told him we were watching the machine to see if we could figure out where the prob-

Management and the Continuation of Chaos

lem was. Perturbed, he answered, "I pay you guys to do something, not just stand there and watch these machines run, so get busy."

This was Carroll's usual response to everything. If all else fails, do something. I had witnessed it my first day in the shop. Even though I had had no idea how the tester worked or even what was wrong, Carroll had me take it apart. His theory was that it was simply dirty and needed to be cleaned. He apparently assumed that any other problem would reveal itself in the process of disassembly.

Over and over again Carroll suggested that dirt was the major cause of a problem. The women used to make fun of him, because whenever he worked on something he brought along a can of WD40 (a spray lubricant and cleaner). "What you got there, magic in a can?" Carol would tease him.

As should be obvious, Carroll's "If all else fails, do something" philosophy conflicted directly with what we learned from Pete. Although conflict seldom rose between them, it did between Carroll and us. One of our first big disagreements occurred when Carroll began accusing us of goldbricking. His solution to this perceived laziness was to increase our duties. He added more machines for me to tend and assigned Bobby a number of make-work projects. Over the course of a couple of months the main responsibility for the SELMs shifted to me. In this way Carroll not only reduced a two-person job to one person, but added more duties as well.

Although the machines were running considerably better and I knew much more about their maintenance, they were hardly self-maintaining. They required constant attention, especially at our increased level of production. So the change in job duties replaced our earlier confusion (which we had mostly alleviated through getting the machines running) with a more advanced form.

A New Kind of Chaos

Another effect of the reassignments was Bobby's increased marginalization from the activities of the floor. As I noted before, Bobby lacked a strong self-image, and his new duties made him even more self-doubting. "Doesn't he trust me anymore?" "What does he think I am?" Bobby would ask. More deflating than being taken off the SELMs, however, were the projects Carroll gave him. In typical National fashion Carroll gave Bobby work which he had no background or inclination for. Worse, he would give Bobby general instructions and then leave him on his own—a kind of openness that meant real problems for Bobby.

For example, the spools of wire used on the SELM were rolled up a ramp to the machine (they were too heavy to be lifted). We had one ramp that we shifted from machine to machine, and it was fairly dilapidated. Carroll told Bobby to make a new one. He did not give him much more instruction than that, and told him to use scrap lumber from the pallets. The lumber used in pallets, however, is green hardwood that is extremely difficult to work with, and we didn't have that much of it. Bobby spent days on the project. When Carroll finally came around to view the results, he was not disappointed but angry. I watched as he told Bobby, "This will never hold the weight," and then proceeded to step on it. Bobby's pride as well as the ramp was crushed.

This happened over and over again. Bobby was constantly set up for failure in make-work projects that had not been carefully thought out. This development, combined with the effect of his removal from the SELMs, made Bobby more frustrated and angry. His work deteriorated further. He started taking days off, and although June, the floor lady, arranged a transfer downstairs, he only lasted a week on the "braiders" and then left National.

Meanwhile, I was beginning to resent that Bobby was doing make-work while I had to keep the SELMs running and learn a

Management and the Continuation of Chaos

new set of machines at the same time. With Bobby no longer involved, Carroll became increasingly involved with my work. He didn't join in the actual repairs, but he was closely monitoring my work and making sure there was always more in the wings.

Carroll's new involvement represented a change, and not for the better. Although Bobby and I had often resented his meddling before, we had needed any help we could get, and Carroll knew as much as we did or more. However, thanks to our experience and training from Pete, we now knew more than Carroll in most areas. His suggestions were becoming less useful, often irritating.

For example, we had a problem with one end of the stripped wire "fanning out" before it reached the applicator. When the terminal was applied, strands of wire hung to the side and the leads had to be rejected. Carroll asked me why the machine was down (I had to be rejected. Carroll asked me why the machine was down. (I had been working on the other machine, which had a less serious problem. I wanted to get it running before tackling the harder job.) "Now if you follow my logic, you can see where the trouble is. The wires are hitting the guard right here," pointing to a place where the conveyor picked up each wire. "All you have to do is fashion a stiff wire or a piece of cardboard to guide the wires over the top of the guard and you'll be all set. It shouldn't take more than ten minutes." In typical fashion he turned around and left, leaving it up to me how to make this custom part.

As time went by, I grew angry at these suggestions. First, they often did not emerge from real understanding of the machines. Second, in their casualness, Carroll implied that the solutions were so obvious that I should have seen them myself. Although I could often identify Carroll's solutions as short term, incorrect, and sometimes dangerous, they put me in a delicate position. If I chose not to use them, I had to have another approach, and a convincing explanation for it. At the same time, if I chose to implement his suggestion, and it either did not work or led to another problem, I was no further ahead. Carroll could stay upstairs or be involved elsewhere, but I had to live with the machine.

Thus I was embroiled in constant negotiation. If I followed Carroll's orders literally, I often failed to solve the problem. But if I neglected to follow them, I risked being labeled insubordinate or (worse yet) lazy. The difficulty over "fanning out" illustrates the dilemma. I took Carroll's suggestion and tried to fashion a piece of cardboard to guide the wire over the guard. It was not as easy as it sounded. The "ten-minute" job took an hour. I found some cardboard and cut a piece approximately to shape, but I ran into two problems. First, I had to fasten it to the machine. The metal was too oily to use tape, so I had to locate a bolt. The only usable bolt was a long distance away, so I had to recut the cardboard. Then I cycled the machine through by hand to ensure that this custom part would not interfere with other moving parts. Unfortunately, this larger piece of cardboard blocked the "jaws" that grabbed the wire. For the next half hour I cut and trimmed three or four different pieces before getting one just right.

The cardboard part succeeded in guiding the wires over the guard (most of the time) and very few ended up at the applicator fanned out. Carroll's solution had apparently worked. Yet the terminals were not being applied any better. Some fell right off, and in others the wire was inserted too far or not far enough into the terminal. Clearly, the fanning of the wires was not the cause of the problem, but a symptom.

I checked the applicator itself, which looked all right, as did the wire positioner. Some careful study pointed to the conveyor itself. It appeared that it was picking up the wires too early, and consequently delivering them too quickly to the applicator. Pete had gone over this repair with us, but I had never done it alone.

It was a major repair, although not as major as it looked. To get at the adjustments for the conveyor, most of the guards (covers) had to come off the machine (like taking off all the fenders of a car). Carroll had made his suggestion for the cardboard attachment at 7:30 A.M., it was almost 2:00 P.M. by the time I had the machine running again. I was pleased with the application of my newfound knowledge, but I knew Carroll would have preferred to solve the problem with cardboard.

The Costs of Autocratic Control

Keeping the machines running on a more regular basis should have made my work less confused and alleviated some of the chaos on the shop floor. Yet given the forces that operated at National, these improvements simply changed the nature of the chaos. I would like to examine the resiliency of chaos at National, and how its continuance was a product of a particular management style.

Some confusion was a function of the general nature of the shop. Materials (wire and terminals) did not arrive on time and the SELMs would fall behind the demand for leads. At other times a part was out of stock or no longer available, which had the same effect. Events like this raised havoc with my day.

There were also more hidden forces that disrupted any sense of regularity. Some of these forces might be seen as economic ones. For example, Carroll's decision to take Bobby off the SELMs might be seen as an economic move. Why employ two men when you can do the job with one? That's simply good business sense.

Yet I would argue that this is good business in the narrowest sense. If Carroll had kept Bobby and me together only a few more months, with the advice and council of Pete we could have significantly improved the general repair of the shop. Even in the short term these improvements would have increased productivity and profit well above the $4.00 an hour National was paying Bobby. Especially in that the work they gave him instead was hardly productive, it made even more sense to leave Bobby where he was. Yet management at National constantly made narrow cost-benefit decisions that scarcely made sense in the short run. However, I would argue that economics was not the sole factor in many of these decisions.

As Bobby and I worked with Pete, we learned repairs on the SELMs that Carroll knew nothing about. If pleased with the results, he saw his shop-floor control receding. I believe that his decision to take Bobby off the SELMs and increase my workload had as much to do with reasserting control on the floor as it did with economics. It is hard to explain his behavior in any other way. One afternoon, for example, soon after Bobby had left National, I had just finished a fairly major repair when Carroll walked by. He pointed out that I had not readjusted the counting mechanism on the machine so it would register. This was true, but compared to the repair the counter was trivial. I may have intended to get around to it, though if I had not it was no major issue. Most of the machines did not have counters anyway. Yet this kind of criticism was becoming a part of Carroll's attitude toward me. It was his way of saying, "If you think you're so good, how come you forgot this?" The more skilled I became, the more accountable I became for smaller and smaller details. But more than accountability, the true issue was control.

I grew increasingly angry at such incidents, and Carroll detected it. He eventually called me into his office for a talk. He told me I had an "attitude problem." "You're getting too possessive of those machines. The other day when I was down there, you wouldn't let me get near the SELMs. Every time I even mentioned something, you almost bit my head off. You're not the only one who knows anything about those machines. Nobody's indispensable, you know. The last guy who had your job thought that he was." Then he told me to post the notes I had taken from Pete once and for all; he wanted to start rotating mechanics on different machines, so that everybody would know a little bit about everything.

I can remember being livid at this suggestion. It made no sense to give all the mechanics superficial knowledge of every machine. As we have seen, the nature of machine repair demanded craft knowledge that was not general in any way. It was based on experience and "feel." If Carroll really implemented job rotation, the shop floor would soon be back where it started from, or even worse.

As I learned more about my job and took more pride in my work, I began to question Carroll's decisions. As his job rotation scheme demonstrates, that kind of pride was not acceptable. This kind of pride needed to be checked, even at the expense of production. Training other mechanics who could do my job was a way to maintain control on the shop floor. The rotation plan, however, proved more difficult than Carroll had expected, mostly because we were too short of staff to train anyone else. Also, though we tried the rotation, it was clear that operating the SELMs for extended periods required more than a list of instructions.

A Changing Management Style

Before proceeding further, it is important to put the management style at National, especially its obsession with control, into perspective. At first glance, it appears to reflect the particular idiosyncracies of management at National. Yet upon closer examination this obsession with control is less a peculiarity of National than part of a general trend in American management over the past ten years.

A Changing Management Style

Although it may seem a big jump from National to General Motors, there are some important parallels for our discussion here. According to John DeLorean, former vice president of General Motors, the hallmark of the successful General Motors corporation built by Alfred Sloan was *"centralized* policymaking and control, and *decentralized* operation. This meant that the operating decisions for the day-to-day running of the business were made at the division level" (Wright, 1979: 7 [emphasis added]). Yet like a number of other American corporations, GM ran into trouble sustaining its high level of profit during the late sixties. Consumers had begun moving to smaller, more efficient cars that General Motors had just begun manufacturing. DeLorean argues that GM missed this golden opportunity, not because of its lack of innovation (there were in fact a number of small cars that had already been designed) but because of a change in its management style: "I found that the fine tuning had gone out of control. As I progressed in the corporation, I watched General Motors' operation slowly become centralized. The divisions gradually were stripped of their decision-making power. Operating decisions were more and more being made on the fourteenth floor" (Wright, 1979: 7).

There is evidence that the increasing centralization DeLorean described has been occurring not only within layers of management, but between labor and management (Bowes, Gordon, and Weisskopf, 1983; and Simmons and Mares, 1983). According to Bowles, Gordon, and Weisskopf (1983), an increase in control on the shop floor was central to this "great repression":

> Between 1948 and 1966, for example, the ratio of supervisory to non-supervisory employees in the private business sector increased by nearly 75 percent—from roughly thirteen supervisory employees per one hundred employees to more than twenty-two. By the late 1960's, nearly twenty cents of every dollar of revenue paid to the private business sector covered the salaries of manage-

Management and the Continuation of Chaos

rial and supervisory personnel (Bowles, Gordon, and Weisskopf, 1983: 74).

The intensification of centralized control has not been without costs. In fact, much of the literature discussing the "superiority" of Japanese to American industry illustrates these costs.[3] Not only have centralized American firms been more inflexible to changes in market conditions, but their productivity and quality have been adversely affected as well: "Capital has begun to win the battle against labor, in short, but it was continuing to lose the war" (Bowles, Gordon, and Weisskopf, 1983: 113).

Carroll's decisions, then, rather than idiosyncratic, are part of a national trend toward increasing shop-floor control. Carroll had won the war against Bobby and me, but chaos was winning on the shop floor.

3. For example, see William G. Ouchi, *Theory Z: How American Business Can Meet the Japanese Challenge* (Reading, Mass.: Addison-Wesley, 1981); Richard Tanner Pascale and Anthony G. Atlas, *The Art of Japanese Management* (New York: Simon and Schuster, 1981); and especially Ezra F. Vogel. *Japan as Number One: Lessons for America* (Cambridge, Mass.: Harvard University Press, 1979).

5. Speed-up and Productivity

THERE IS LITTLE DOUBT THAT INDUS-
try in the United States has become significantly less productive.[1] This recognition of our lagging productivity has spawned
voluminous discussions and hundreds of "productivity improvement programs," as companies both small and large struggle to
stay afloat.[2] National was not immune from the pressure and the
management was constantly pushing for higher productivity.

This chapter focuses on two such attempts: a physical speed-up
of the SELMs, and a new procedure and tooling intended to speed
production of the three-wire assembly. A careful look at these two
incidents offers some important insights as to how the management
at National viewed the problems of productivity. As well, it suggests some reasons why other productivity improvement programs, although more sophisticated than the ones at National,
have proved unsuccessful.

Speed-up on the Line

Although it would intensify later, the speed-up on the line actually
began while Bobby and I were still working closely with Pete on

1. This has been argued by authors across a broad political spectrum. For example, although they differ greatly about the solution to our productivity problem,
Samuel Bowles, David M. Gordon, and Thomas E. Weisskopf, *Beyond the Waste
Land* (New York: Anchor Press/Doubleday, 1983), and Ira C. Magaziner and Robert B. Reich, *Minding America's Business* (New York: Random House, 1983) agree
on our serious decline in productivity.

2. For a summary of a number of these programs, see John Simmons and William Mares, *Working Together* (New York: Alfred A. Knopf, 1983).

Speed-up and Productivity

the SELMs. About this time Carroll brought in a new man to work with us. Mike was in his late twenties and, like me, was one of the "old timers" in the shop. His job was to repair another high-speed cutting and stripping machine and the sewing machines that were giving us quite a bit of trouble. From the very first it was obvious that Mike was an excellent mechanic, and although he was working at minimum wage he had more experience and better skills than I.

We quickly grew to like each other, and although we did not work on the same machines, we helped each other as much as we could. More important, Mike and I shared a general viewpoint on the shop, whereas Bobby and I never did. Because National was Bobby's first "real" job, he assumed that National was like everywhere else. Mike knew better. He had been "in wire," as he called it, for over ten years. The last five years he had been employed in a large wire mill in town. He had been involved in organizing the union there, and was ultimately fired (although illegally) for union activity.

Coming from a large, established shop that was less involved with high-tech, Mike was shocked by some of the procedures at National. That we shared a similar view of National made us fast friends and inseparable in the mill.

Besides repairing the sewing machines and the Eubanks (the other high-speed cutting and stripping machine), Carroll had Mike work on making changes on the line. Carroll's main concern was the way materials moved from one task to the next—for example, from the blockers to the sewers. "These girls are wasting a lot of time getting up and looking for a box of work," I overheard him telling Mike, "and they always end up talking to someone in the process."

Carroll was correct in his assessment of the disorganized way that materials moved from one station to another. Sometimes the sewers would get assemblies neatly stacked in a small box. At other times the assemblies would be thrown in a big box which the women asked us to lift for them. Each time a sewer started a new box, she would take out a few handfuls of leads and organize them on her table so she could sew them in rapid-fire succession. Different women approached this task differently, but everyone counted the number of leads they finished so that their productivity rate could be computed.

The experienced sewers also did a spot check on the blocking and the leads themselves to make sure they would pass inspection before they went ahead and sewed them. Because we always had new blockers it was not uncommon to find errors. Since the sewers were the next station along the line, they would often catch these errors before it was too late. These were some of the ongoing decisions the womens' jobs required.

Carroll's idea was to have Mike construct special sized boxes that would hold a given number of assemblies. These would be counted once by the blockers, and therefore would not require other counts. He also wanted Mike to construct a series of chutes and trays in which the boxes could be inverted, positioning the work so that little adjustment would be necessary. Like many of Carroll's ideas, this made sense in principle. Although the women enjoyed stretching their legs or having a cigarette, they did not like the confusion that accompanied a search for materials.

Mike had been in the shop only a few days when Carroll had him cutting up cardboard boxes and fashioning chutes out of an old eaves trough and cardboard. (Mike himself was not very happy with the whole project. "Boy, if the guys back at the other shop ever heard what I was doing, they'd roll over and die".) Even if Mike had understood the shop better the project was doomed to fail.

Speed-up and Productivity

Jerry-rigged out of cardboard, with less than a few hours spent in design, the project had little chance of survival. Mike also had to endure insults from the women (as I had in the beginning) when they realized how ridiculous the project was.

What particularly troubled the women was that the project proceeded with no input for them. Carol, one of the sewers, told me, "I know what they're trying to do here, and if they'd ever ask me, I'd show them what to do." They never asked. She described her idea of extending the benches, which now could hold only a small number of leads, so that the sewers could spread the leads out and get them in order. But the work went on around her as if she wasn't there.

I suspect that workers in many firms have faced similar situations. For example, Ruth Cavendish discusses a similar situation in a considerably larger shop:

> Although we were the only workers with practical experience of working on the line, our views were not taken into account. Changes were made, new designs and machinery introduced with no regard for us. The engineers never had to sit down and use most of their jigs and were often clueless to how they worked in practice. Most of the women could have told them how the machinery could be made more comfortable, which jobs went best together, and how the line could work more efficiently. But no one ever asked us (Cavendish, 1982: 107).

The Forgotten Insight of Taylor

As we have seen, the women on the line do more than just perform menial tasks. Their craft knowledge, learned over time, could be a valuable resource when making improvements. The importance of craft knowledge in many ways forms the basis of Taylorism:

The Forgotten Insight of Taylor

> The ingenuity of each generation has developed quicker and better methods for doing every element of the work in every trade. Thus the methods which are now in use may in a broad sense be said to be an evolution representing the survival of the fittest and best of the ideas which have been developed since the starting of each trade (Taylor, 1911: 31).

Taylor himself was a trained craftsman and consequently recognized the importance of these "rules of thumb," as he called them.

Yet the recognition of workers' craft knowledge was only part of what became the Taylor system. Although Taylor had great respect for "rules of thumb," he was also critical of them. His major objection stems from their "unsystematic" or "unscientific" nature. The function of management under his system was to "gather together all of the traditional knowledge which in the past has been possessed by the workmen and then . . . classifying, tabulating, and reducing this knowledge to rules, laws, and formulae which are immensely helpful to the workmen in doing their daily work" (Taylor, 1911: 36). Once this knowledge was systematized, it was management's task to "scientifically select and train, teach and develop the workman . . . and . . . heartily cooperate with the men so as to insure all of the work was being done in accordance with the principles" (Taylor, 1911: 36).

As both Braverman (1974) and Clawson (1980) argue, the influence of Taylor on American industry and management should not be underestimated:

> (1) he produced by far the best analysis of the existing situation, an understanding of the nature of the problem confronting employers; (2) he developed the solution for the problem, an alternative means of organizing and structuring the productive process and the relations of production; and (3) he was the most impor-

Speed-up and Productivity

tant person directing the implementation of the policies he proposed (Clawson, 1980: 202).

However, although a number of large industrial concerns implemented a Taylor system, not even a sizeable minority of American industrial workers were affected. For workers employed by the thousands of small, localized manufacturers like National, Taylor had little impact. Though he prided himself on being both theoretician and practical man, Taylor's major influence was as a thinker.

Although I believe that he overstates his point, Richard Edwards argues that "If we look at Taylorism as a management practice rather than an idea, the promise was never fulfilled. For one thing, the system was complicated and employers often grew impatient long before the final elements were ready to be installed" (Edwards, 1979: 101). Edwards' choice of the word "impatient" is especially apt. Taylor's system is based on a meticulous attention to detail. It was not based on a manager's or engineer's master plan, but began with a detailed inventory of workers' knowledge. I suspect that it is precisely at this point that managers and engineers grew impatient, and that this counter-trend in American management prevented Taylorism from being more thoroughly adopted.

Managers and engineers have always doubted how much knowledge workers have. That managers have the power to enact changes on the shop floor has led them to believe that they are the best equipped to judge what changes are needed and how they should be made. Managers' belief in their superiority stems from a number of factors. First among them is a lifelong separation from the workers. Although the distance has greatly increased since Taylor's time, workers and managers have never occupied the same social world. This separation of the classes has contributed to the stereotypes of workers as having little intelligence or skill. Second, managers' belief in the superiority of their knowledge is a result of how Western scientific society has defined knowledge. According to this conventional view, knowledge is abstract in nature and takes the form of a general scientific law.[3] It leaves very little room for knowledge resulting from concrete, practical experience.

Given this prevailing notion, it is difficult for most managers to appreciate the kinds of practical knowledge workers have acquired through years of experience. Furthermore, it tends to reinforce the belief that managers, like the scientist looking for the general law, through their theorizing have the answer to how the shop floor could be better organized.

This tendency has been further exaggerated by changing patterns in management. First of all, few of today's managers come off of or have any background on the shop floor and are even more removed from the world of workers than their predecessors. Equally important, despite the growing number of managers (relative to workers) those involved in production may actually have decreased. As we move into a so-called "post-industrial" world of ideas and finances, the new manager is in marketing or finance, not production: "Such managers tend to speculate in financial strategies and operate at great distance from production, which they view as an operating expense that can reduce profits. . . . The product becomes secondary" (Melman, 1983: xiv, 20). This trend further exaggerates the distance between workers' shop-floor

---

3. For a good summary of the "positivist" view of science, see Gerard Radnitzky, *Contemporary Schools of Metascience*, 3rd ed. rev., 3 vols. (Chicago: Humanities Press, 1970).

Speed-up and Productivity

knowledge and the abstract, financial knowledge of today's managers. As interest in production dwindles, workers' knowledge of that process becomes less valued.

Thus I would argue that one of Taylor's fundamental insights—the notion that workers' knowledge is the place to begin any production reform—has been forgotten. On the other hand, those aspects of the Taylor system that stress management control of the shop floor have been most thoroughly accepted. Such was certainly the case at National. Carroll's refusal to even consult with (let alone understand) the women on the line marks a fundamental departure from the basic principles of Taylorism. It was obvious that he thought he had the answer to how the flow of materials could be improved along the line. Although this attitude may be exaggerated at National, recent ethnographies of the workplace suggest it is widespread. Descriptions of an automobile factory (Linhart, 1981), an electronics manufacturer (Cavendish, 1982), and in light manufacturing (Pfeffer, 1979) reveal some interesting similarities. First, to a surprising degree workers were left on their own to figure out how to perform their job. All of the participants had to struggle by themselves, with some help from other workers. Though Linhart worked in a large automobile factory, his description of the first days on the job is reminiscent of my own experience at National:

> My work will consist of preparing the windows, that is to say, fitting them with a rubber gasket. I've got a kind of powder, like talc, to prevent the rubber from slipping. I've got a mallet. You have to aim accurately so that the shape of the rubber fits the window exactly: if you don't get it right the first time it becomes creased or stretched, the rubber comes off at the curved parts, and you have to do it over again. The red-haired man does two windows as a demonstration, asks me if I've understood, informs me

90

in a grumbling voice that the work is piece-work and that I have
to do at least three hundred and twenty windows a day. After
which he strolls off, without even watching me attack my first
window. Not curious (Linhart, 1981: 33–34).

This hardly sounds like the ideal Taylor had in mind. "Scientific"
management is indeed a part of the modern workplace, but there
are many more ad hoc procedures than people suspect. Houbolt
and Kusterer offer evidence from a number of different workplaces,
and conclude: "We have been looking, but so far have been unable
to find a single place where any of these Taylorist principles are
followed. . . . Not a single instance has been found where management attempts to tell their workers *how* to do their job instead
of merely *what* to do" (Houbolt and Kusterer, 1977: 6). Although I
believe they overstate their case, workers' knowledge generally re-
mains an untapped resource.

The Japanese Contrast

The last few years have seen an explosion of published materials
on Japanese industry and management.[4] The new conventional
wisdom declares the Japanese industrial system superior to the
American, and points to the success of their superior products in

4. The three most important popular works include: William G. Ouchi, *Theory Z: How American Business Can Meet the Japanese Challenge* (Reading, Mass.:
Addison-Wesley, 1981); Richard Tanner Pascale and Anthony G. Athos, *The Art of
Japanese Management* (New York: Simon and Schuster, 1981); and Ezra F. Vogel,
Japan as Number One: Lessons for America (Cambridge, Mass.: Harvard University Press, 1979). When I refer to the "popular" works on Japanese management, I
mean these works in particular.

Speed-up and Productivity

the American market. Fascination with the Japanese is not limited to industry and management. As John Woronoff writes, "Admonitions to 'learn from Japan' have been offered for crime prevention, education, social and political harmony" (Woronoff, 1983: 272).

Despite the continuing popular acclaim for things Japanese, some recent literature recommends a more tempered enthusiasm.[5] First, Japanese success may be less widespread than first believed. In *Japan's Wasted Workers* (1983), Woronoff argues in detail that success has been primarily restricted to large manufacturing firms. His description of backwardness in most offices and white collar jobs in both the public and private sectors provides a shocking qualification to Japanese success.

There is also increasing evidence of considerable disparity among workers in general industry. Although images in the media suggest that most Japanese workers are employed in large corporations (with the famed "lifetime employment"), the reality is quite different. In part, large Japanese firms have been successful at the expense of smaller ones, many of which, like National, act as subcontractors:

> The use of subcontract employment is widespread in Japanese
> industry and has a long history. Its importance in steel has grown
> in recent years to the extent that nearly half of the workers at
> most major steelworks are outside employees. The largest subcon-
> tractors are designated "associated enterprises" and are fully inte-
> grated into the operations of the primary employer. As one de-
> scends the hierarchy of subcontractors, wages, job security,

5. See Jon Woronoff, *Japan's Wasted Workers* (Totowa, N.J.: Alanheld, Osmun, 1983); John Junkerman, "The Japanese Model," *Progressive* 47 (May 1983): 21–27; John Junkerman, "Blue Sky Management: The Kawasaki Story," *Working Papers* 10 (May-June, 1983): 28–36; and Satoshi Kamata, *Japan in the Passing Lane* (New York: Pantheon, 1983).

working conditions, and status fall. At the bottom of the ladder, older workers toil at menial and dangerous tasks for about one half of the pay of top-class employees (Junkerman, 1983a: 33).

Moreover, there is evidence that working conditions may not be idyllic even for full-time employees of the major Japanese firms. Although there appear to be institutions for the participation of Japanese workers (i.e., quality circles) there is growing evidence that the workplace is largely managed by a strict authoritarianism. For example, in *Japan in the Passing Lane* (1983), Satoshi Kamata reports that authoritarian control not only existed on the shop floor at Toyota, but extended into company living quarters and the private lives of its workers.[6]

There is additional concern that, like its counterparts in the West, the Japanese system is threatened with shrinking growth rates. The phenomenal rate of growth has been slowing steadily, and "consensus" and "cooperation," the hallmarks of the Japanese system, may be less achievable in an era of shrinking resources (Junkerman, 1983b).

Despite these caveats, the success of Japanese industry—undoubtedly among the most productive in the world—cannot be denied. It is important for us to understand the reasons behind that success, though understanding will not come easily:

Explaining the heady success of Japanese manufacturing has, in recent years, virtually replaced baseball as our national pastime. The trouble is, however, that American managers cannot agree among themselves on the rules of this new competition, the cur-

---

6. It must be noted here that the title of Kamata's book, *Japan in the Passing Lane*, is unfortunately misleading. It was originally published in Japan in 1973 under a more appropriate title, *Automobile Factory of Despair*.

Speed-up and Productivity

rent score, or even the precise kind of game in which they are involved (Wheelwright, 1981: 67).

The popular literature suggests that the major difference between the American and the Japanese systems lies in their basic philosophy. Whereas the American system is founded on conflict, competition, and suspicion, the Japanese system is founded on loyalty, cooperation, and trust. It is surprising how much space is given to accounts of underlying philosophy. Consider Ouchi, author of the bestselling *Theory Z* (1981): "The thought of mixing practical business matters with pie-in-the-sky concerns may seem strange, but popular beliefs aside, philosophy and business are the most compatable of bedfellows" (Ouchi, 1981: 131). He continues, "So important in terms of building Z companies is applying the principles expressed in the philosophy to everyday working life" (Ouchi, 1981: 132).

Yet upon closer inspection the main difference between American and Japanese management systems has little to do with overall philosophy; nor does the Japanese philosophy seem to be the major reason behind their success. As Woronoff writes, "Putting as much stress on a company philosophy as Professor Ouchi does is absurd" (Woronoff, 1983: 282). In fact, the reasons for Japanese success seem less a function of things Eastern (including philosophy) than the perfection of practices adopted from the West:

> Contrary to public opinion, this evolution has not come about
> through the use of techniques like quality circles and advanced
> techniques like robots. What Japan has created is the factory of
> the present, operating as it should. Japanese managers have never
> stopped emphasizing the basics. To them, every stage of the man-
> ufacturing process—from product design to distribution—is
> equally important. They constantly work to improve equipment

94

design, inventory control systems, and workers' skills through cooperation at all levels. The ultimate goal? Perfect products and error-free operations (Hayes, 1981: 57).

Japanese success, therefore, is based on techniques close to those suggested by Taylor. Rather than the product of an Eastern ethic, these involve a meticulous attention to detail that Taylor suggested. This is in part possible because there are significantly more engineers in Japanese companies than in American ones.[7]

American commentators continue to note the careful attention Japanse industry gives to the production process. Steven Wheelwright observed that "the dedication of Japanese manufacturers proves the value of strategic operations research" (Wheelwright, 1981: 67). Or as Andrew Weiss expresses it, "Superior productivity in Japan does not hinge on the 'oriental' style of management or on Japanese corporate culture, but rather on the mundane decisions managers make" (Weiss, 1984: 121). Thus the Japanese have been more successful than Americans in implementing a Taylor-inspired system of production:[8]

> The Japanese approach to cost reduction was once the classic American pattern. It was the one that gave American industry its world supremacy in production (Melman, 1983: 199).

7. See Andrew Weiss, "Simple Truths of Japanese Manufacturing," *Harvard Business Review* 62 (July-August 1984): 121.

8. The influence of Taylor on Japanese management is not as indirect as it might appear. His books sold over 1.5 million copies in Japan, and his ideas were quite popular in the first part of the century. For more on Taylor's direct influence in Japan, see John Simmons and William Mares, *Working Together* (New York: Alfred A. Knopf, 1983), pp. 96–99; and Robert Cole, *Work, Mobility, and Participation* (Berkeley: University of California Press, 1979), pp. 135–37.

Speed-up and Productivity

The application of Taylorism to Japanese management may appear surprising at first. Taylorism, after all, is usually associated with the strict control of workers, whereas Japanese management has been perceived as more cooperative. Although growing evidence about shop-floor conditions suggests that the Japanese system is less cooperative than first thought, it is true that worker input is taken seriously (Junkerman, 1983a and 1983b; and Kamata, 1983). But the Japanese understanding of the term "cooperative" differs from ours. It is not so much that managers cooperate with workers (in terms of shop-floor control, for example), but that workers cooperate with managers (by giving them suggestions and ideas how production could be better organized). Then, as envisioned by the Taylor system, these ideas and suggestions are systematized by managers. As Robert Cole has written:

> Among corporate management in the industrialized market economies, there is no doubt that it is the Japanese managers, above all, who maintain most of their traditional managerial prerogatives and hold firm to the reins of power. Worker participation, worker commitment, company training, and so on, must all be understood in this context. For those committed to democratizing the firm this hardly represents an ideal to be emulated (Cole, 1979: 252).

The cooperation between Japanese labor and management on the shop floor has often been misunderstood by those who argue for the application of Japanese techniques to the United States. For example, American labor unions are roundly criticized for their confrontational stance; the cooperative behavior of the Japanese is held up as a corrective example. In *Toward the Next Economics*, Peter Drucker presents a Japanese union official who is appalled by American unions. "But yours [unions] fight the company. How can they not know that for anything to be good for the company's employees, it has to be good for the company?" (Drucker, 1981: 174).

Comparisons of this sort convinced many that United States productivity has fallen behind largely because "stubborn" unions have failed to cooperate with management.[9] Hence the call for union concessions at the bargaining table. I would argue, however, that it is mistaken to cite the bargaining table as the major area of cooperation. More precisely, the main site of cooperation in the Japanese system is the shop floor, where workers, managers, and engineers work together. Workers' knowledge is both acknowledged and integrated into design changes. The kind of cooperation that exists within management itself is equally vital. In *The Art of Japanese Management* (1981), Pascale and Athos compare the Japanese company Matsushita with the American firm ITT. The major managerial difference is that Matsushita builds a management team over time and with great care promotes individuals from within, while ITT recruits heavily and constantly to lure the "best and the brightest" into the company. In sharp contrast to Matsushita, there is constant competition at ITT as individuals jockey for position. Further, ITT's chairman of the board hardly fostered a spirit of cooperation: "Part of what made Geneen's system work was fear. Fear of individually being caught uninformed, of being humiliated in meetings, of being punished" (Pascale and Athos, 1981: 71).

Few would argue that there is much cooperation between American workers and managers on the shop floor—or between managers themselves. I suggest that it is pointless to urge cooperation at

9. For example, see Robert Kaus, "The Trouble with Unions," *Harper's* 266 (June 1983): 23–35.

Speed-up and Productivity

the bargaining table when it does not exist at these more fundamental levels. No number of concessions at the bargaining table will alter the conflict on the shop floor. Only when workers' knowledge is respected and integrated into shop-floor practices will we see the growth of "cooperation."

This discussion of Taylorism and Japanese management puts Carroll's behavior in perspective. That is, National is squarely in the American tradition—it sees solutions to production problems as the exclusive responsibility of mangement—and stands in stark contrast to the Japanese. In what follows, we will see how this autocratic management style contributed to the failure of two attempts to increase productivity.

Speed-up on the Line

Although Carroll abandoned his cardboard boxes and chutes, he did not abandon his intentions of speeding up the production line. His focus, however, shifted from a concern with the flow of materials to a specific station on the line, the blockers. I think that Carroll correctly assessed that blocking was the slowest and most troublesome station along the line. It took twice as long as any other job, and consequently involved twice as many workers. It was also the most despised job by workers, and consequently caused the most problems.

As discussed earlier, blocking was assigned to new women on the floor. If they survived long enough (most did not) they took another job as soon as one opened. The constant turnover resulted in a slow production rate of assemblies, too many of which would later be rejected.

There were four pneumatic (air) machines on the shop floor. Two were mounted on the blocking tables and two hung around the workbench and the shelves in various stages of disrepair. We had no idea what they were for. At one point, when Bobby needed a large metal plate to flatten some rivets, he pirated a plate from one of these machines. When Carroll happened by, he was incensed. "Don't you know what that is? Who ever gave you the impression that you could take that apart? What do you think that was, junk?" His violent reaction made better sense when we realized that Carroll had been involved in the design of the machines. It turned out they were intended to speed the blocking procedure.

A few months later, while Bobby was working on Carroll's special projects, one of his jobs included adjusting these air blockers. First you loaded them with four blocks; the fifth block pushed the first in front of a three-pronged fork. At that point you inserted the three wires into their proper channels, although not with enough force to complete the blocking operation. Hitting the footswitch released air that moved the fork forward and completed the operation. Another block was inserted and the operation repeated. For what seemed like weeks Carroll had Bobby testing and adjusting, grinding and testing, and so on.

When Bobby left the floor and Carroll became concerned that I wasn't busy enough, he assigned the task to me. As with other projects he assigned me, I held off as long as I could because I could see that the machines were sure losers. He and I played a cat-and-mouse game on these assignments. He'd say to me, "So how are you coming on the [X]?" I'd usually answer with something like, "Gee, I've been real busy with the [Y], but I'll get to it as soon as I can." I knew that these blockers had become important when he finally demanded that I work on them.

Although I did not generally respect Carroll's mechanical abilities, I was impressed by the design and construction of the blocking machines. They were simply and sturdily built. The major problem lay not in the machine itself, but in the fork that inserted the

Speed-up and Productivity

leads. Because the channel in which the wire was inserted was not much larger than the terminal, and also because of the terminal's shape, pressure could not be applied simply in its middle, but needed to be applied equally at both ends. Worse, in the center of the channel (on the top) was a ridge that extended one-third of the way down. Carroll's approach was to have Bobby grind the fork thin so it would not approach the ridge at the top. However, this strategy resulted in a fork so thin that it bent with time; also, its edges became sharp, which scratched the block.

It was clear that grinding would not solve the problem, so with Carroll's permission I started designing a new fork. Instead of making it thin to avoid the ridge in the center of the channel, I designed it much thicker (so that it would not bend) with a groove in each prong of the fork for the ridge. The goal was to use the ridges to guide the blade in and keep it away from the side of the channels, thereby preventing it from scraping the block. Carroll approved the design and I sent the sketch to the local machine shop, which began working on the prototype.

While we were waiting for the prototype, Carroll assigned me to another project. At the opposite end of the line from the blockers were the singers, who passed a heat gun over the completed assemblies to shrink the thread around them. They lined up thirty or so assemblies on an aluminum tray that reflected the heat, and passed a heat gun back and forth over the assemblies. You had to use enough heat so that the thread would shrink securely but not turn brown.

Carroll came up with an idea to suspend the heat gun from the ceiling. "Just go get one of those screen door springs and fasten it to that beam up there. That should take the weight off the gun and make it a lot easier on the girls." It sounded simple enough, but (as so often) it took all day to complete. The spring was easy enough to find but attaching it to the heat gun so that it would point in the right direction proved no easy task.

We had a good time on the floor while I worked on this set-up, because the women were as skeptical as I was. They kidded me, but mostly we kidded about Carroll. "He'd hang anything from the ceiling if you'd let him," said Linda, one of the singers. "I'd like to hang him from the ceiling," said Carol, who watched all this from her sewing machine.

After much laughter, I finally got the heat gun hooked up. I adjusted it to a number of different heights at Linda's suggestion, but we couldn't make it work correctly. It held the weight of the gun and worked fine in the center of the tray, but as you moved to either end the arc lengthened; a singer would have to pull the gun down to the proper height. We could not solve this difficulty. Maybe a different kind of spring would have helped. There was also the problem of what to do with the gun while loading and unloading the tray.

We worked on this set-up for the rest of the afternoon without much luck. Linda felt it was easier to do the job the old way. She preferred to lift the heat gun than fight with the spring. When Carroll came around and asked how she liked the set-up, she told him. He took it as a personal attack; "You girls don't appreciate anything I do for you. I was only trying to make it easier on you." Linda, who was fed up with the whole affair by now, barked back at him, "It's got nothing to do with making it easier on me, you just want me to work harder."

This sorry situation is typical of the contradictory positions in which workers often find themselves when involved in changes on the shop floor. Carroll had never bothered to talk with Linda, let alone ask how she thought her job could be improved. She is a opinionated woman, and I am sure she had some ideas.

Speed-up and Productivity

Instead, Carroll turned her job upside down and then was surprised to find her angry. He often commented on how inflexible the girls were, and implied that his solutions would be perfectly good if the "girls" were not so set on their ways. In this way bosses impose new procedures on workers without consulting them, and then accuse the workers of being uncooperative and adversarial.

We forgot about the singeing experiment, because the next day the prototype blocking fork arrived from the machine shop. It looked very good. The only noticeable error was that the hole for the mounting screw was counter-sunk on the wrong side, which meant it could not be mounted in the air machines. At first I thought this difficulty would prevent us from testing the fork. But I remembered when the blockers' hands grew very sore Carroll let them use a small tool on a handle that pushed each lead in separately. We decided that if we mounted the fork on a handle and made a board to hold the blocks secure, it might allow us to make a test. The women on the line were more receptive to the idea of a hand tool than to Carroll's air machine. The hand tool also seemed to circumvent the major drawback of Carroll's machine, which was the difficulty of loading the leads into the blocks.

We had the women try it out on a few hundred assemblies, and it looked great. There was hardly a scratched block among them. I rounded off the ends of the fork a bit more and then worked on designing a more permanent set-up for the fork. We tested a few hundred more assemblies, and they looked even better. The whole floor was excited. Although the blockers would feel differently later on (and contrary to Carroll's belief in their inflexibility), they were genuinely excited. The new design held the promise of eliminating the problem of perpetually sore fingers.

No one was more pleased than Carroll. Although he still hoped to make things even faster by using his air machines, he was surpisingly flexible about the forks as hand tools. This "success" on my part improved our relations greatly. He had given me more independence on this project than ever before, and it seemed to be paying off.

The blocking fork was passing its test nicely and Carroll told me to order six more of them. While waiting for their arrival, we had a number of "sessions," as Carroll called them, to determine the best (i.e., most productive) way to set up the new blocking operation. There were two aspects of these sessions relevant to our present discussion. First, they took place almost exclusively in Carroll's office rather than on the floor near the prototype set-up or by the blockers. Second, our talks essentially amounted to theorizing on what would be best, and ended with Carroll sending me off with something to try. Like the experiment with the heat gun, none of the women on the line were consulted, and in many ways this was the fatal flaw that brought a promising change to an unsuccessful conclusion.

We finally agreed to extend a blocking board that contained a channel to hold the blocks firm along the entire length of the table. We attached a box at one end to catch the blocked assemblies as they "fell" off the table. Because the board extended the entire length of the table, the women would no longer have stacks of leads in front of them. Instead, we set up three trays behind the blocking board. We also attached a box at the other end of the table to hold blocks so that the women would not have to bend down.

We timed the one blocker using the prototype, and she was almost doubling the usual rate, a phenomenal improvement in any kind of manufacturing. News was beginning to spread around the mill. The next day the general manager and the vice-president, who hardly ever appeared on the floor, came upstairs to look at the operation.

Speed-up and Productivity

We were full of excitement when the call came from the machine shop that the additional forks were ready. I quickly made some handles for them. Before the day was out, we had three of the four set-ups working. The first day's results were impressive. We lacked an exact count, but it looked good. There appeared to be no scratching, and we left work feeling proud of our accomplishments.

The Troubles Begin

The next morning, however, brought disaster. One of the sewers noticed that the center lead was not pushed all the way in in nearly one-third the assemblies. It was easy enough, however, to give it a small push into its locking position. When I compared the forks we had received with the prototype, I noticed that the center prong was slightly shorter than it should have been. The solution was to file a small amount from the outside prongs, so that the center would push the lead far enough in. It was a disappointment, but hardly a serious set-back.

More serious, however, was the discovery of a significant number of scratched blocks. Although we had tested the prototype with some caution, we had not tested the new forks. Clearly something was wrong; production could not continue like this. There were, however, differing strategies about how to solve the problem.

June, the floor lady, would have liked to forget the new blocking tools altogether. Carroll's involvement in the operation, however, took away much of her power on the floor. Carroll, on the other hand, saw the problems as minor, and wanted to continue using the tools while we solved the problems we were having. The women on the line were ambivalent. Many liked the tool, but others liked it less as it became the source of confusion on the line.

I would have preferred to test the tool carefully, as we had done with the prototype, before using it in production. Carroll, however, won out, although we scaled down the operation slightly while I worked on the problems. I had solved the difficulty of the center lead, but no matter how smooth I made the blades they still scratched the blocks. However, becoming involved with the women using the tools turned up some interesting findings.

First, in not a single instance was the blocking board being used in the way we had intended. Working the full length of the table turned out to be too cumbersome; also it required too much force to push the blocks off the end of the table. Most of the women were using less than half the board. This allowed them to place the leads in stacks directly in front of them, as they had always done, instead of using the trays we had built in back. Yet these variations from the original design were not causing our difficulty.

The crucial factor was the tool itself, which turned out to be much more sensitive than I imagined. At my workbench, without the pressure of making what was now a double-rate, I inserted the tool in the blocks slowly and carefully, and almost never scratched the blocks. Similarly, the woman who had used the prototype over several weeks had developed a fairly smooth approach.

I discovered that the majority of women used a jabbing motion as they rushed to produce this required lot of assemblies. This motion sometimes scratched the blocks. The women had received no training beyond a ten-minute explanation by Carroll, and consequently each had developed her own style for using the set-up.

When Carroll heard this, his first tendency was to blame the women on the line. "You can't trust some of those girls to do any-

Speed-up and Productivity

thing. I don't know how some of them walk around without bumping into things," he said. This was typical of his normal way of apportioning blame. Yet I was coming to learn how even the most sturdy machine could be disrupted by the smallest factor. A reality of the factory setting is that machines break down and go out of adjustment. Carroll knew this as well as anyone, but it was not his first reaction to a production difficulty. He more often assumed that the problem was human error, "one of those girls again."

An incident with the heat guns highlights Carroll's attitude. They burned out regularly, and Carroll had John, one of the mechanics upstairs, repairing them. We had a large order to get out one afternoon and one of the singers brought me a gun she said was not hot enough. I took it upstairs, and because John was out for the day Carroll gave me another from John's bench. I took it downstairs, but Linda, the singer, complained it had the same problem. I took both to Carroll. He plugged them in and said they were fine, and that Linda probably had not opened the vents enough. This went back and forth between Linda and Carroll—and I went up and down stairs with the guns.

Finally June called Carroll on the phone. "I've got an order to fill and you won't get it unless you get us a heat gun that works." Only when Carroll came down himself and compared the heat gun to others did he admit there was something wrong with it, and that Linda was not at fault. This happened over and over. Carroll's first reaction was to blame the worker and not the machine, although his own experience proved that the reverse was usually true.

Carroll behaved exactly the same way over the blocking tools. He preferred to ignore the obvious fact that the fork had structural problems. Merely because I could use it at a leisurely pace at my workbench did not prove it was correctly designed. That is the challenge of tool design. It is not enough to make a tool that works in a test situation; it must stand up to the rigors of production.

Moreover, we must be careful in assigning blame to the women workers, because they had never been trained for the job. Obviously, Carroll felt that training them was unimportant, that the tools were self-explanatory. His attitude about training in many ways follows from his low opinion of workers' craft knowledge. Simply show the operators how to use the machine (turn it on, shut it off, supply it with the necessary materials, and so on) and set them about their tasks. However, this arrangement will only work in an ideal factory where machines do not wear out and materials are always consistent. That not being the case at National, it was clear that training was needed on these new set-ups.

Blaming women left Carroll in a curious position. If the women could not be changed through training (although they might be changed through the threat of dismissal), then the only alternative was to change the machines.[10] And that's what Carroll decided to do. He interpreted my request for training as an admission of failure. If the set-up for blocking was perfect then it could be operated by anyone, regardless of skill or training. Carroll's response was, "I want these things to work so anybody can use one, I don't care if she's the worst kind of klutz. I don't want to have to spend hours coaxing them to do it right."

Carroll's statement makes it apparent that he wanted not only to increase production, but lower the skills needed for the job. Despite his continual threats to replace the women with someone off

10. The threat of dismissal was Carroll's major way of "motivating" the women on the line. He saw the problem as one not of training (he thought the women knew what to do) but of motivation. Thus he used the threat of dismissal to make the floor more productive.

Speed-up and Productivity

the street who could do their job better, he knew it was not yet possible. A "skill-less" operation, however, would give him considerably greater control over the women than he currently enjoyed. Recent literature on the labor process argues that desire for control is often an underlying motive for the implementation of a new technology.[11]

The End of a Dream

The next few weeks were in many ways similar to my initial weeks at National. We continued to fine tune the forks (although we did nothing about training), but we never stopped using them long enough to test them adequately. These weeks were an unending series of crises. I would adjust the forks; we would think we had the problem solved; the next day we would discover hundreds of damaged assemblies. My relations with Carroll began to break down as we continued to differ over strategy. The blockers also began to take sides. Most of the older women grew to dislike the new set-up. The newer blockers, however, were still hopeful of going home without sore fingers.

We had our usual deadlines to meet, and assemblies began to bottleneck at the blockers. In addition, we had scores of boxes that required painstaking checks to see if the assemblies would pass inspection. June, whose main responsibility was to make sure that orders were done on time, grew more impatient day by day. Carroll remained as obstinate about doubling the rate. It all, however,

---

11. See the works contained in Andrew Zimbalist, ed., *Case Studies on the Labor Process* (New York: Monthly Review Press, 1979).

The End of a Dream

came to a sudden stop. One day Carroll called a meeting of everyone in the cafeteria. He informed us that one of the companies we supplied had reduced its order for the next two months and that he would have to lay off about half the women. They would be laid off approximately along lines of seniority but if anybody wanted to, they could take a voluntary layoff. I was suprised how well most of them took it. One of the older women later explained to me that this sort of thing happened two or three times a year. Apparently they had grown accustomed to the instability of working for a subcontractor with a varying workload.

A few of the younger women did not take it so lightly. Most had not been working long enough to collect unemployment. I saw one who had been working on a SELM throw a handful of leads into the machine and curse at Carroll. "I was just starting to get my bills paid, and this no good son-of-a-bitch lays me off with a one-day notice." Many could not afford to wait for a call-back, and took work elsewhere.

Carroll talked to me at the workbench and told me that the layoff would not affect me. He planned to shut down both SELMs, but that would give me a chance to do some maintenance which I could not do while they were running. I was pleased to have the extra time (especially after the ordeal with the blocking tools) without the pressure of production, but I asked whether it would not make sense to keep one SELM running to build up inventory. Carroll said no.

One consequence of the lay-off was that all the women (with the exception of one) who had been blocking lost their jobs. The older and more experienced women who were sewers and singers took over the blocking job. There was no mention of the new blocking tools. The women went back to their old ways, and although the

Speed-up and Productivity

blocking boards and trays remained in place, it was as if the whole experiment had never occurred. A sense of calm descended over the shop. Neither SELM was running, which made the floor ghostly quiet. The great promise and the great confusion over blocking was over.

A Desperate Attempt

The layoff ended as abruptly as it had started. After eleven days, Carroll not only called back all the women (at least those who had not taken work elsewhere) but added some as well. The company that had reduced its order had turned around and doubled it. We immediately fell behind on the SELMs even though they were running fairly well. We could not keep up with such high demand. I often thought back to those eleven days when we could have run at least one of the machines at a leisurely pace.

During the previous month Carroll had talked about putting a larger pulley on the SELM to physically speed up the machine. I was dead set against it from the beginning. I thought Carroll would be more cautious after the disaster with blocking, but he pushed ahead. I assume he was under pressure from upper management. Although he believed that the SELMs could stand the speed-up, the new pulley seemed a strained attempt to convince upper management that he could increase production. It was a desperate attempt.

Carroll had calculated that the machines would run one-third faster. However, we could not locate the pulley he wanted, and ended speeding up the machine almost by half. After all the months of growing accustomed to the rhythm of the SELMs, the accelerated speed was awesome. The heads of the women on the line turned one by one to see what was going on. I fully expected a part to fly off the machine, though miraculously it did not.

I watched as Carroll and Nick, the time-study man, figured what the machine could produce in a single day. The potential quantity was astonishing. They were visibly excited. Their calculations, however, were based on several ill-founded assumptions. They had taken the hourly rate for the machine (which had been increased to 4,800 leads per hour) and multiplied it by seven (eight hours minus a half-hour lunch and two fifteen-minute coffee breaks). Although their experience should have told them differently, they somehow forgot that the SELMs seldom ran for more than a few hours without a breakdown or set-up change.

A few weeks earlier the time-study man and I had played around with the figures on the average daily demand for leads from the SELM. Using the manufacturer's figure of 3,200 leads per hour, we calculated that we could theoretically exceed the average daily demand for leads by running each SELM only four hours per day (actual running time). Nonetheless, despite pushing the SELMs seven hours a day we were still always behind, which suggests how much down time was involved in our operation.

That Carroll chose to accelerate the machines rather than minimize down time indicates he only identified part of the problem. Rather than creating a steady level of production, Carroll achieved unpredictable bursts accompanied by enormous repair difficulties and huge quantities of scrap. The result was more chaos on the shop floor.

I suspect that Carroll is not the only manager unaware how much of the time machinery does not run. Managers get sold machinery that promises certain production rates, yet often fail to in-

Speed-up and Productivity

vestigate how well actual production measures up. This oversight is not restricted to small shops. Melman (1983) discovered that it was common to find advanced, numerically controlled machine tools running only 55 per cent of the time, despite the manufacturer's promise of 95 per cent availability (Melman, 1984: 109). The significant amount of time machinery lies out of operation provides another way in which our industrial workplaces prove less rational than conventionally believed.

I am sure I spoiled some of Carroll's fun by predicting doom for the revamped SELM. Despite my pessimism the machine ran fairly well for a solid week (I even lost a bet with Carroll on this score). We then put a larger pulley on the other SELM. This machine was older and presented additional problems, but after a time it also ran.

In the coming weeks, however, I watched the situation deteriorate. The machines continued to run at incredible speed, but the amount of scrap was phenomenal. We slowed one of them down to solve this problem, but the inconsistency did not change. We finally called in Pete.

Pete blew up when he discovered what Carroll had done and threatened to revoke the service contract. He said that people had put on different pulleys before—but only to slow down the machine to improve consistency. We spent a number of days trying to figure out the source of the current problem, only to discover it deep within the machine. The SELM was run by a large electric motor which transferred power to the conveyor by two shafts and a series of chains. Each shaft had a channel on one side, as did the pulley that fit on the shaft. A "key" fit into the "keyway" that held the pulley firmly on the shaft. We discovered that we could hold the shaft and move the pulley one-quarter inch. When we disassembled it we saw that the increased force on the machine had enlarged the keyway and battered the key.

To make this repair required the disassembly of the machine's basic drive-train. Even Pete was on new ground here. Getting all the parts we needed was impossible. We ended up jerry-rigging a solution as best we could, but the machines never ran as well again.

Beyond a Mechanistic Solution

Carroll's speed-ups were ultimately unsuccessful because they took a mechanistic approach to the complex issue of productivity. They were mechanistic in one sense because Carroll saw the SELMs and the production process in general as overly simple and rational. Moreover, he always assumed that problems with productivity were primarily technical, requiring solutions like speeding up a machine. Yet the blocking experiment made clear that the technical and social aspects of production are inseparable. The new blocking tools would only have been successful if coupled with training—and if the women on the line accepted them. That Carroll ignored these social elements in production ultimately undermined his efforts. Bowles, Gordon, and Weisskopf write of the "mystery" of productivity: "We suspect that the key to the mystery lay in understanding how the people in the production process—workers, managers and others—affect productivity independently of the mechnical or technological environment in which they work" (Bowles, Gordon, and Weisskopf, 1983: 125).

Finally, although it has been popular as well as easy to blame workers for our sagging productivity, this chapter has demon-

Speed-up and Productivity

strated that managers make an important contribution quite beyond what their workers feel or do. As Roger Zanger of the Work in America Institute has observed, the productivity index "does not show how productive workers are, only how productively employers use them" (quoted in Simmons and Mares, 1983: 11). As long as management insists on absolute control of the shop floor and fails to build on workers' knowledge, it is difficult to see any solution to our present crisis in productivity.

6. Quality Control

THE CONTINUING DECLINE OF BASIC

industry and the intrusion of foreign products into our markets have stimulated much discussion about the quality of American products. "Many consumer advocates, government bureaucrats, management consultants, business writers, and even business executives are now convinced that 'Made in Japan' has replaced 'Made in USA' as a label guaranteeing quality" (Leonard and Sasser, 1982: 163). Many commentators would not take the argument quite that far, but there is general agreement that the declining quality of American products is one of the major factors behind our industrial crisis.

The business community apparently agrees with its critics. Hardly a new or an improved product is introduced without some assertion of its improved quality. Advertisements portray teams of engineers and workers working hard to locate problems that would later cause trouble, or inspecting products, and the like. Quality has even become part of company slogans ("where quality is job one"; "We really sweat the details at . . ."). One cannot help wonder, however, if this seemingly endless stress on quality perhaps conceals flaws of a different sort.

This chapter examines the issue of quality by looking at a "quality improvement program" that was instituted at National. It reveals how management perceived creating quality items, but also how this concern with quality was tied to increased productivity and shop-floor control.

117

Quality Control

A Quality Program

Although National possessed nothing so formal as quality circles, the general cultural preoccupation with quality had trickled down to our management. We constantly heard about the possibility of losing orders if we didn't do our work well. Carroll was especially proud that our floor had the best record of any supplier (at least according to him) and indicated our order would grow if we kept it up. The implication was that increased orders would make our work more steady, and we might even expect a pay raise.

Since Carroll was the production manager, however, he was not primarily responsible for quality control. That was the job of Nick, the time-study man. Indeed, in many instances Carroll and Nick took opposite sides on an issue. As in most workplaces, there was built-in friction between production (quantity) and product quality. Carroll had to make sure that our orders were completed in the time specified, while Nick had to make sure they met the company's specifications. This division of labor was not always harmonious, and the workers at National were often caught in the crossfire.

Soon after the dust had settled from the failed blocking experiment, Nick hired a new head inspector (until then we did not have a head inspector) and instituted a new quality control program. The new inspector was a middle-aged woman who had no previous experience "in wire," although she had been an inspector at one of the large industrial concerns in town. She arrived on the first day significantly more dressed up than the other women in the shop, and she carried a clipboard, stopwatch, and micrometer. These tools never left her side while she was at National.

Needless to say, she was resented by the women on the floor even before she arrived. They were always suspicious of someone new, and even more so when they discovered that the new inspector had no experience in wire. June, the floor lady, felt the same: "Anybody in wire will tell you, it's different. It's not like when you're working in metal or steel. Wire stretches and gives, and you can't go around like it didn't. Ask anybody in wire, they'll tell you."

The decision to hire an inspector without experience is partly a consequence of management attitudes discussed in the previous chapter. Management felt it less important to hire someone who really knew our production procedures than someone who had general abstract knowledge about quality control and could use the appropriate scientific instruments. Their choice of an outsider is also important. They were opting for someone who could be objective (in the narrow sense), who could evaluate our products without being affected by personal relationships or sympathies with the women in the shop. In fact, the inspector's sympathies were more likely to lie with management than with the workers.

The women at National realized all this from the first day and were not about to stand for it. Unlike the blocking experiment, and partly because of it, they knew they had little to gain from a new head inspector and the program that came with her. The new blocking equipment had appealed to the women because it promised to make their jobs less taxing. There was no such carrot in the present situation to lure them into cooperation.

From Quality to Workmanship

Mary, the new head inspector, first turned her attention to the SELMs. They were still running at the faster speed when she arrived, and consequently with more problems than usual. She started by learning the specifications for the leads. The specified

Quality Control

tolerances (the amount a measurement is allowed to vary) were still plus or minus one-sixty-fourth of an inch (1/64″), which, as we discussed previously, were totally unrealistic for our operation. The machines when new were designed to run at plus or minus one-thirty-second of an inch (1/32″) but in actuality had been running at plus or minus one-sixteenth of an inch (1/16″), a margin totally acceptable to the companies that bought our products. But it was not good enough for Mary. She had been hired to improve quality, and with "born again" enthusiasm she began making life miserable for me and the SELM operators.

As we discussed earlier, part of the skill of the women on the line was this constant negotiation of variances from ideal specifications. Because of the ad hoc production process and consequently the unevenness of the products at National, choosing what was good, and what was not, was not always an easy process. It was not just that the women were more lenient, or that they were not concerned with the quality of what they produced. In fact, I was surprised at how much pride they took in their work. One could see it in the way Alice neatly stacked the leads in her boxes after they came off the SELM. In fact, during the course of an incredibly boring day of inspecting 15,000–20,000 leads, one of her only joys was to see the leads stack up beside her.

What our new inspector failed to understand was that the decision to pass an item through inspection could not be based on the mechanistic application of an ideal. A dogmatic adherence to the official specifications would close National down. In fact, this was beginning to happen. Mary kept shutting down the SELMs because they were too far off tolerance. This was creating resentment on the floor. Alice, June, and I had a pretty good idea what the companies who bought our products would accept, and we knew that Mary was being overly precise. More upsetting, we learned she was going over our heads and reporting our reticence to the general vice-president (apparently the main instigator behind this quality program). Even Carroll was angry. "Squealing" on another worker is simply not acceptable in the working culture. June commented, "Even Carroll and I can work out our problems without having to go upstairs, and I'll be damned if I'll let her do it." It was becoming clear where our new inspector's loyalties lay.

Judging from their behavior, neither Mary nor upper management expected quality to result from negotiation or cooperation on the shop floor. On the contrary it had to be imposed on workers from above. Management expected to impose standards and supervise the workers in order to improve their sloppy work habits and lack of concern with product specifications.

Ironically, while our new inspector was concerning herself with whether the leads conformed to tolerance, we were having a serious, recurring problem with the wire. The wire was always the weakest link in our production. From my first day in the mill, we faced problems with wire that broke constantly, was too large or small in diameter, had a loose braided fabric, was uneven in texture and color, and so on.

Over the months we had instituted an inspection of the wire as it came onto the floor. Ellen, one of the inspectors, checked the braid, the stiffness of the wire, and a host of other characteristics. This inspection, however, was not always effective. Ellen might reject a spool of wire and send it downstairs (where it was made), but often the people downstairs would simply reel off a few hundred feet and sent it back upstairs. If Ellen was too rigorous, Carroll or one of the bosses from downstairs would push the spool through inspection anyway. June, Alice, and I complained, but nothing ever changed.

Part of the problem was that we were in effect buying the wire from ourselves. Most of what we manufactured downstairs was sold outright. One of the men, however, told me they had much

Quality Control

more stringent standards for the wire they shipped out, especially to some customers. So they sent us the short pieces and the marginal wire.

I suspect that this is not an uncommon occurence in many kinds of manufacturing. Part of keeping productivity high and waste low is to devise a way to pass your marginal products down the line. Because supplying our floor with a mediocre product was good for the company (although not for our floor), we made little headway in improving what we received for the SELMs.

Partly out of desperation (and partly out of revenge), we complained to Mary about the wire. Inspecting the wire, however, proved a different matter from measuring the tolerance on the leads. We watched with amazement when she tried to measure the wire with a pin-style micrometer. Measuring woven wire like ours with a pin micrometer (which was designed for measuring metals) was like measuring a pillow with a yardstick.

Our main problem was that some wire was simply too stiff, which had something to do with how the jacket was woven. We watched for days as Mary twisted the wire, took it apart, measured it, ran up and down stairs—all of this to arrive at proper "specifications." But we did not need formal specifications to tell us that certain wire was bad. Alice especially, after years of experience, had an incredibly sensitive touch, and she could detect if a thread was missing in the weave or if the wire was oversize merely by feeling it.

We were not worried about *identifying* "poor materials," which was easy; we wanted to *do* something about them. Our inspector saw it differently. She wanted firm, scientific standards by which to reject or accept a given spool. In theory, this idea is not necessarily bad. However, measuring the quality of some items is more difficult than others. Even our "simple" wire would require a number of interactive measurements. There may be a machine to test the stiffness of wire, but National was surely not prepared to buy it (I will say more about the use of scientific instruments later; the important point here is that we could identify poor material without additional "tests").

This example demonstrates that management at National equated quality with workmanship. In other words, shoddy products result from poor workmanship. According to this logic, our floor had not been conforming to the specified tolerance, and for this reason our products were poor. I would not deny that workmanship is often a problem—but that was not the case here.[1] Moreover, as long as the focus is on workmanship, "quality" is something that happens after the fact, instead of being part of the production process all along. Surely it made sense to ensure that we received high quality wire, but our new inspector preferred focusing on our conformance to over-rigid tolerances.

I would suggest that at least three important factors in addition to workmanship contribute to the quality of a given product: 1) the quality of the raw materials; 2) the design of the product; and 3) the speed and the quality of the machines in production. Our example makes clear that the first factor, the quality of materials, played a major role in our final product—our problem was not our inability to distinguish bad from good material, but our inability to improve the raw materials we received from our own company.

Design is also vital to the overall quality of a product, although it was not particularly a problem at National. Many of our products had been designed by the companies that bought them; also, most were simple. In major industries, however, product design can be a major drag on quality. Perhaps the best example is the auto industry. The business community itself is beginning to ac-

---

1. In those instances where workmanship is a major factor in the quality of an item (as we discussed in Chapter 5), it usually reflects a worker's lack of training, not his lack of concern.

knowledge the direct relationship between design and quality (Judson, 1982: 93–97).

The third factor, the speed and quality of the machines, was very significant at National. The simplest, most efficient way to improve the leads would have been to slow the SELMs to their former speed. Over and over again our dilapidated machinery contributed to poor products. Thorstein Veblen wrote some seventy years ago (as if he had National in mind):

> The instinct of workmanship, on the other hand, occupies the interest with practical expedients, ways and means, devices and contrivances of efficiency and economy, proficiency, creative work and technological mastery of facts. Much of the functional content of the instinct of workmanship is a proclivity for taking pains.
>
> *The best or most finished outcome of this disposition is not had under stress of great excitement or under extreme urgency* (Veblen, 1914: 213 [emphasis added]).

Consequently, most of the factors involved in producing a quality item are not only out of workers' hands, but determined before they ever touch it. It is not enough simply to fine-tune aspects of workmanship; rather, quality must be a concern from the very design of the product. Finally, an almost exclusive focus on workmanship can lead—as in this example at National—to little more than "blaming the victim."

Quality Control and Control in Quality

The concern with quality (that is, workmanship) seems to be everywhere in American industry. We might ask what functions the various quality improvement programs really serve. There are probably two general reasons why American industry supports them. First, they play an important rhetorical function, especially in advertising. Second, they help management shift the responsibility for quality off themselves and onto workers. Yet these two general reasons do not explain why shops like National institute quality programs.

Besides these general concerns, I would argue that "quality control" programs have become so popular because they not only are concerned with product improvement, but are concomitantly avenues for increasing productivity and exerting more discipline on the shop floor. Discipline was certainly a part of the quality program at National. We were never under a more watchful eye than Mary's. We knew she was reporting variances from the specification for the leads on the SELM; what else was she reporting to the general manager? It was not that we had anything particularly to hide, but if she had misunderstood how to apply the specs, she probably would misunderstand why someone was talking to another worker, or why I was sitting at my workbench. We were nervous about her presence on the floor because we felt that our behavior would be taken out of context.

It was especially troubling that Mary circumvented the normal production hierarchy, even though this practice is typical of many quality improvement programs where a consultant or a special employee reports directly to someone higher than he or she would normally report to. It may allow more top-level management involvement in the programs, but it also encourages more surveillance on the floor. For example, it was clear that Mary had become an important information source. On one occasion Carroll came to the floor and reprimanded an inspector and the operator on a SELM for talking. Since it was early in the morning, and Mary had

Quality Control

been the only person to leave the floor, there was little doubt she had given Carroll the information. One could understand (although perhaps not accept) taking information upstairs if it was even remotely connected to quality; however, that was not the case here.

The concern for improving quality often results in the closer monitoring of workers by inspectors, machines, and also other workers. Parker and Hansen (1983) suggest one consequence of instituting Quality Circles: "The older workers are now 'slow', and employees who didn't mind carrying them in the past now see them as a drag on productivity. Production workers begin to bad mouth 'do-nothing' skilled workers" (Parker and Hansen, 1983: 35). This quote leads nicely to our second point: that quality improvement programs are also often tied to improving productivity. The increased monitoring was the worst part of Mary's presence on the floor. We doubted that she would have much effect on the quality of products, despite all her tinkering, but nobody liked the way she kept careful track of production records—and, at least informally, of how hard we were working on the floor. Although high productivity and high quality are in many ways antithetical, quality programs often link them together. In that they focus primarily on workmanship rather than on quality, they might be more appropriately called "Productivity Circles."

Being more concerned with discipline and productivity than with the improvement of quality, the quality improvement program actually worked to undermine worker confidence and pride. As has been clear, workers knew what "quality" meant in their jobs; even if they could not effect improvements, they knew exactly where the weak points were. That the new head inspector did not understand or respect this knowledge, but instead focused on trivial issues, had a profound impact on the workers at National.

Quality Control and Control in Quality

As I mentioned, Alice could tell what was wrong with the SELM wire simply by feeling it. That was only one of a number of skills she had developed over her years at National. Because of this skill, she resented Mary coming around with her micrometer and vernier calipers (another measuring instrument). "I don't know what she thinks those things are going to tell her. If she'd just open her eyes she'd see this wire is no good." Yet, because Alice could not use a micrometer, she was mystified by it, which led to her gross over-estimate of its importance.[2] Despite her overall healthy disrespect of scientific gadgetry, the micrometer was something that better educated and more powerful people used. Thus she often forfeited her skepticism of it. For example, we were talking about another inspector one day and Alice said, "She's good. She can even read a micrometer and everything."

The use of formal tests in quality programs generally demoralizes workers. Although at one level the workers are suspicious of them and see their connection to increased production and discipline, because they often do not understand the tests, the tests take on an overly important role. A skilled worker may really know what making a good product entails, but it is very difficult to hold on to the validity of that knowledge in the face of a "scientific" test—especially one you do not understand. Michael Lewis quotes an interview with an electrician, Eddie Finn, that demonstrates this ambivalence towards formal knowledge:

> Being an electrician is no cinch—you've got to know alot, as much as any electrical engineer or maybe even more, because the electrician is out there on the job and he's got to make decisions

2. For a discussion of mystification, see Erving Goffman, *The Presentation of Self in Everyday Life* (Garden City, N.Y.: Doubleday, 1959).

which come up that the engineer never thought about. So let's get this straight right away, you don't just walk off the street and say you're an electrician. No way!

That's why we've got this test for people who want to join the union. There's a written part and you have to come in for an interview. The written part was put together by a bunch of engineers, so you know it's no phony deal (Lewis, 1978: 148).

Although Eddie, much like Alice, is skeptical of engineers' knowledge (he perceives his craft knowledge as more developed), he turns around and accepts it as a certification of how to do things the right way.

As we have seen, workers possess craft knowledge that would seem worth tapping in any attempt to improve quality. However, to the extent that management prefers abstract tests and procedures, it ignores this craft knowledge and erodes its workers' pride. This in turn further alienates workers from quality improvement programs and lessens the chance for any real improvement.

Quality and the Obstruction of Pride

Mary continued devising tests, checking our work, reporting information upstairs, and constantly shutting down the SELMs. She was stopping them even after the machines had been slowed down and ran more like their old selves. We could see the growing resentment in Carroll, who saw all this as an intrusion into his production schedule.

As the weeks went by and the anger grew among all of us, Mary became more and more ostracized. The women mocked her by impersonating her walking around with her clipboard. At lunch they refused to make room for her in the cafeteria. Finally, after less than

Quality and the Obstruction of Pride

a month on the job, she resigned. She submitted a lengthy letter of resignation, and although we never saw a copy, June told us what it said. In many ways it confirmed what we ourselves felt about the shop. Although Mary criticized us for being stupid and uncooperative, she criticized management even more. She thought the whole operation was a mess, and that management should get someone who really knew what they were doing to straighten it out. We could not have agreed more.

Like always after these fiascos, we settled down to our old way of doing things, glad that Mary had not been more successful. For months afterwards, when we discussed whether an item would pass inspection, someone would mimic her. Oddly enough, resentment toward her grew stronger after she had been gone. As Alice said, "It was like a slap in the face, her coming around like that and telling us that we weren't doing our job right. Why, I'd like to see her sit here year after year like I have, having them changing all the time what is good and what isn't and all the time never getting any decent wire. It wasn't fair." Alice felt sure she understood what quality was all about, but she doubted that management or the inspectors did. In the final analysis, then, management's quality programs proved to be obstacles rather than roads to better-made products. Furthermore, the mechanistic ways they were implemented caused unnecessary resentment on the line.

I was surprised that Alice still cared about her work at all. The rules always changed, the machine broke down, Carroll or Nick would come down and chew her out, the wire would break—all this on top of a job that was tedious and noisy. Yet when the SELM broke down, it was as if her best friend was sick. When it operated incorrectly, she often became angry with it. At first I thought she was angry at me, but after a while I realized she blamed the machine for producing poor quality leads. But despite it all, week

Quality Control

after week, month after month, she sat under the fluorescent light inspecting the leads and stacking them perfectly in cardboard boxes.

One cannot help but wonder why she does it. Unfortunately, I think the first tendency is to see it in the most negative fashion. ("How could she be so stupid, not only to do this job year after year, but to continue to do it well?") Unfortunately whenever we see someone doing manual work over time, we tend to see that person as somehow simple-minded, and we reduce him or her to the stereotype of the "happy worker" (Swados, 1957: 65–69). I am sure that asked about her job, Alice would respond that she liked it. Yet this response means both more and less than it seems. What it does *not* indicate is, "Yes, I like my job, it's the job I've always dreamed of, and if I had my life to do it over I'd like to have this job again."

Although I never talked to Alice about her past, I am sure she once had dreams of becoming more than a shop-floor worker at National. Yet she ended up working on a SELM, and it is precisely because she has that job that she likes it. Nora Watson, who was interviewed by Studs Terkel in *Working* (1972), observed that "most of us, like the assembly line worker, have jobs that are too small for our spirit. Jobs are just not big enough for people" (Terkel, 1972: xxix). Yet few people accept that reality. Most of us then make our job more than it "really" is.[3] Studs Terkel touches on this point in his introduction: "They all in some manner perform astonishingly to survive the day" (Terkel, 1972: xviii).

What I think is often misunderstood is how in fact people on the shop floor, like the women at National, survive. Perhaps one of our

3. For a more complete analysis of our reconciliation with failure, see Michael Lewis, *The Culture of Inequality* (Amherst: University of Massachusetts Press, 1978).

basic means of survival as a species is our ability to make meaning-less situations meaningful. Among prisoners in concentration camps, children in abusive homes, and citizens in the midst of national terror are those who can miraculously create meaning and order in order to survive. No less miraculous are those who spend the better part of their lives on stools, at machines, blocking leads, and the like. And despite what managers may feel about America's declining quality, most workers want to create this meaning by performing their job as well as they can. Barbara Garson concurs:

> I have spent the last two years examining the ways people cope with routine and monotonous work. I expected to find resent-ment, and I found it. I expected to find boredom, and I found it. I expected to find sabotage, and I found it in clever forms that I could never have imagined.
>
> But the most dramatic thing I found was quite the opposite of noncooperation. *People passionately want to work* (Garson, 1975: xi).

Over the months at National, despite constant changes on the line, the failure to recognize workers' knowledge, the speed-ups, the quality experiment (and all the other experiments), I was as-tounded that most women continued to care about their jobs. Somehow, despite all the chaos, they were able to create a sufficient amount of meaning to keep them going. Some of it was created by "ritualized routines" (see Chapter 3) which they followed, no mat-ter what was happening on the floor. But most importantly, they derived meaning from their daily tasks. Things were best for them when they produced decent quality goods without too much con-fusion. The leads piled up on the shelves, the women could choose the best box from them, they stacked them neatly, rejected those

Quality Control

that were bad—and this was enough to keep everybody going. Garson described her experience in a number of different workplaces:

> Somehow in the unending flow of parts and papers, with operations subdivided beyond any recognizable unit of accomplishment, people still find ways to define certain stacks of work as "theirs"; certain piles as "today's" and "tomorrow's".
>
> Almost everybody wants to feel she is getting something accomplished—to see the stack of paddles, the growing pile of dark meat, or to master the job blindfolded since there's not much to master the other way (Garson, 1975: xi).

These small satisfactions were upset when machines broke down or when Carroll disrupted production with one of his schemes. Those were the hardest days for all of us. Without the pleasure of watching our completed work pile up, the day became exactly what it was: routine, long, and boring. Many people believe that the "routine" is the worst possible aspect of work in a mill; in actuality, it enables people on the line to develop ongoing survival strategies. The constant break in routine, on the other hand, made working difficult.

We were luckier than some. Rather than facing what seemed an endless mountain of work, we sent out shipments constantly; for this reason we worked under daily deadlines. Admittedly, I watched on occasion as women hid assemblies, slowed down, and in less obvious ways worked so as to prevent an order from being completed. However, that was the exception. For the most part the women worked hard to get orders out on time.

Sometimes we would race against the clock to see if we could finish a job in time, or even more quickly than expected. Although these games have been a permanent feature of the industrial work-

Quality and the Obstruction of Pride

place, they are still misunderstood by many. Burawoy, for example, sees production games as a way in which workers exploit themselves into producing more "surplus value." The shop which he examined in *Manufacturing Consent* (1979) paid according to piecework (ours did not), but he argues that the increased production that stemmed from production games was not motivated by economics: "Making out (making over your piecework rate) cannot be understood in terms of the externally derived goal of achieving greater earnings" (Burawoy, 1979: 85).

Although Burawoy makes a passing observation that games may play a role in "reducing the strain of an endless series of meaningless motions," he fails to incorporate it in his discussion (Burawoy, 1979: 78). In effect he offers a cost-benefit analysis, and in those terms he can see games only as part of workers' false consciousness. As Clawson and Fantasia argue in their review of *Manufacturing Consent*, "It is characteristic of Burawoy that he sees making out in 'either/or' terms: either workers make out for the money, or they do so for the game" (Clawson and Fantasia, 1983: 676). However, when one considers all the factors involved, including workers' motives, a different conclusion emerges.

For example, one hot May morning Carroll came to us with a number of small stripping and cutting jobs. We considered this "chicken-shit work" because it took more time to set up the machine than to run the job. We also knew that these small jobs meant that things must be going slowly. But Mike and I worked as hard as we could for two solid days to do these jobs faster than Carroll expected. I probably never worked that hard in my entire life. We finished in less than half the time it was supposed to take, and because terminals had to be applied to the wires by hand, the floor was completely backlogged. At one point we even ran out of the

Quality Control

trays to stack the orders in. We spent the next day bragging about how much we had done—and the last two days of the week recuperating from the hard work.

From one standpoint our behavior seems clear evidence for Burawoy's thesis. How could we be dumb enough to work so hard just to confuse Carroll, a man whose opinion we did not particularly respect? We certainly did not gain anything out of it economically. Yet our activities look considerably different from the perspective of the shop floor. Contrary to what Burawoy intimates, we knew we were working harder than we needed to, and that we were creating "surplus value." But we hardly thought of it in those terms. The point is, however, that you cannot go around the shop and survive as a simple, economically rational, worker. Instead, we played the game for noneconomic reasons. First, we enjoyed disrupting the floor. Although Burawoy sees these games as only retrograde, they are in many instances very analogous to slow-down on the job. In the same way, they are the result of workers' intentions to purposefully disrupt the normalized routine on the shop floor.

But more than an assertion of our power in the shop, the games we played were time markers, a way to break up events and distinguish one day, one week, one month from another ("Hey, remember that time we did a week's worth of work in two days? That was last month, wasn't it?"). The games were mechanisms of survival, especially for the women on the line, and were more important to them than the economics of production patterns. Perhaps Burawoy sees it as economically rational to do as little as possible on the job; however, for the women at National they could not survive in such an endless world without meaning. Working "is a search, too, for daily meaning as well as daily bread, for recognition as well as cash, for astonishment rather than torpor; in short,

Quality and the Obstruction of Pride

for a sort of life rather than a Monday through Friday sort of dying" (Terkel, 1972: xiii).

To return to our discussion of quality and the production of quality items, rather than seeing quality as antithetical to a worker's maximization of self-interest, this discussion has illustrated how workers (even more than companies) need to produce quality items as a way of surviving the inhumanity of most shop floors. At National it remained their major avenue for producing meaning in what was an extremely chaotic existence.

Yet, if I were to conclude here I would be giving a neat, but inaccurate account of National (and, I would suspect, most other mills). Workers do not always work their hardest to produce high quality items. First of all, they did not in some mechanical fashion always work as hard and as well as they could. Like all of us in our work, they sometimes take extra breaks, have "bad" days, and grow less careful than they should be. Yet none of this offers serious impediments to high quality work.

There are also incidents of a different character. I witnessed workers purposely making bad leads, breaking machines, hiding bad work, letting inferior work pass inspection, and so forth. Yet for the most part these were not acts of uncaring or malicious individuals. Indeed, the framework that we have built thus far gives us a way of "understanding" this kind of behavior.

Perhaps the most important factor in making these actions intelligible is to understand their timing as well as their history. For example, I once watched Bobby use a ten-pound copper mallet to smash a machine part that cost hundreds of dollars to replace. This sort of incident often finds its way into the popular press ("Worker Smashes Machine!"). I do not condone Bobby's action (at the time I was furious with him) but a series of events that led to the incident

Quality Control

does much to explain it. He was originally called to make a small adjustment on the depth of the machine's applicator. It was a simple adjustment accomplished by loosening a single screw. In a normally equipped shop it would have been a five-minute job, but Bobby could not find the proper screwdriver. We searched all the toolboxes, but the screwdrivers were either too large or had been ground at the ends. Bobby asked Carroll if he could buy a screwdriver at the hardware store down the street. Carroll refused and told him to grind one of the ones we had. Bobby tried, but ended up stripping the scewhead so badly that nothing could get it out. Then Carroll came to the floor and in typical fashion chewed Bobby out in front of everybody. After Carroll left, Bobby brought the applicator over to the bench and smashed it. The context of an act explains a lot.

I could give a number of examples about workers who could take the frustration no longer, who met one too many roadblocks, who smashed a machine, did poor work, or just stopped caring. It is extremely hard to predict when a given individual will break. It is surprising that some of the older women like Alice had not broken long ago. But the important point is that Bobby did not smash the applicator as an attack on quality. Events like this occur out of frustration with a chaotic workplace that erects barriers to quality and undercuts workers' pride.

Conclusions

This discussion offers a different picture of workers and their relationship to quality than is presented in the popular press. If anything, I found the workers at National overconcerned with quality and productivity. Quality and productivity are in many ways essential for workers' survival in the workplace. The real problems did not lie in shoddy workmanship, but in factors for the most part outside the workers' control (materials, design, and speed). Furthermore, even when workers intentionally produced inferior goods, their acts were not functions of carelessness or unconcern, but of frustrations presented by the company.

7. Conclusions and Possibilities

IN THIS CHAPTER, I WOULD LIKE TO BRING together a number of separate points that I have been making about chaos on the shop floor at National. It is these points that, taken together, create the overall conditions that I have been describing. The incidents of the speed-up, the quality control program, and my description of the ad hoc nature of production illustrate the kind of conditions workers labored under at National. However, together they paint a much more complete and dramatic portrait of how these conditions adversely affected workers at National.

No Peaceful Goodbyes

When my projected stay at National was about over, I gave Carroll one month's notice. I later found this was highly unusual at National. Most workers gave no notice; those who did gave only a week or two. Carroll was not surprised. "I sort of figured you wouldn't stay here much longer," he said. He did not ask me to stay, or try to keep me by offering more money. I had received one 50 cent raise my first month, and although Carroll had promised me another raise on three occasions, it had been turned down each time by management.

I gave the overly long notice for two reasons (in addition to inexperience). First, I wanted to ease my transition out of the mill. At the time I was informing workers that I was conducting research and also requesting interviews, and I wanted to be seen as depart-

Conclusions and Possibilities

ing in a responsible fashion.[1] Second, the long notice would provide plenty of time to train another person. I knew from personal experience how difficult it had been to learn my job, and I wanted to give my replacement a head start.

Despite these good intentions, my exit turned out anything but smooth. Who was to replace me became an issue. Carroll very much wanted Mike to take the job. Mike wanted it too, but not the way it was offered. Carroll wanted to give Mike my job, not bring in another man to do Mike's present duties, and only raise his pay by 25 cents per hour. Mike was only lukewarm about the proposal.

For two weeks Mike and Carroll sparred with each other. Mike would take the job, then he would refuse. Carroll said he would try to get Mike more money, but my experiences had taught Mike what to expect from that.

Meanwhile, Carroll had me breaking Mike in. Under the circumstances, Mike was hardly enthusiastic about learning the intricacies of the SELMs. Also, though he was a fast learner, he had other duties as well, and it was difficult to find time to show him some of the main problem areas on the machines.

As we moved into the third week, Carroll became more agitated. He could sense Mike's ambivalence toward the job, and it seemed to him that I was not diligent enough in my training. His solution was to take me off the SELM, give the main responsibility to Mike, and call me in if Mike had any problems. This solution, however, proved no solution at all. Mike had not yet learned enough to keep

---

1. It is important to note the reactions of the workers at National when I informed them I was "writing a book about working in the mill." To my surprise I received not a single negative comment. By far the most common response was, "Now make sure that you write how bad this place was." Linhart (1981) and Cavendish (1982) had similar experiences.

the SELMs running. Moreover, Carroll assigned me to rebuild a series of machines I had never worked on before. He thought I was taking it too easy, in the guise of training, and decided to get some "real" work out of me.

I was more than mildly upset. I had given extra notice so that I could train my replacement. But this move by Carroll not only prevented me from training someone, it penalized me (through extra duties) for trying to act responsibly.

Both Mike and I protested. When I was called to the personnel office after coffeebreak, I had a pretty good idea what was coming. I was told in carefully phrased wording that "National was refusing the option of keeping me on during my two-week notice period." I was to pick up my tools and leave at the end of the day. I had been fired. Everybody knew what had happened when I came back on the floor, and the first thing Mike did was go to Carroll's office and quit. Carroll made no attempt to keep him on, although Mike was the only other person who knew anything about the machines.

Probably all workers want to feel indispensable ("How could they get along without me?"). Both Mike and I felt that way as we sat in a bar across the street from the mill, proud of our courage, but embarrassed that we were both out of a job. But there was more than a belief that our importance had not been acknowledged; we were appalled at the waste and irrationality of National.

Mike and I were not really indispensable, provided that Carroll and the rest of National were willing to live with six months of chaos until a new person learned the job. Mike kept repeating over and over how stupid they were not to have trained somebody before letting us go. Carroll, too, had never insisted that I post the notes that I had taken from Pete, and they went home with me in my toolbox. Everything I had learned would have to be relearned by the next person in the same ad hoc fashion that had characterized

Conclusions and Possibilities

my training. Ironically, Pete had been called back to his home office and was being replaced by someone who, although a good engineer, knew nothing about the actual repair of machines. Earlier that day Pete and I had watched as his replacement and Mike struggled with a repair that had become routine to Pete and me. Now Mike was leaving too. It seemed like such a waste for new people to struggle at learning what we could easily teach them.

Apparently none of this bothered the management of National. Although we felt they were being irrational and self-destructive they did not seem to care. It did not make sense. On the other hand, it made as much sense as Carroll's speeding up of the SELMs, or the implementation of the quality program.

The Normalization of Irrationality

Throughout this study I have described a number of incidents that appear irrational—not only from a worker's perspective, or from management's, but from anyone's. Why would National ignore the service contracts on the SELMs, fire me and also let Mike go, or lay off most of the women only to re-hire them two weeks later? I think our first impulse is to view these occurrences as mistakes on management's part, and attribute them to ineptness. On the most superficial level, then, National needs a competent management team. Yet our analysis brings us to a very different conclusion.

I was never a big fan of National's management, especially Carroll, my immediate supervisor. His views and decisions were often the opposite of mine. Yet, although I have stressed how workers were caught in the web of chaos on the shop floor, it would be misleading not to recognize that middle-level management is caught in the same web. This is neither to approve nor condone

The Normalization of Irrationality

Carroll's bad decisions, but it is important to see them as more than the product of his own competence. For example, in the case of the speed-up on the SELMs, it was clear that he acted under pressure from upper-level management. I suspect that Carroll would have liked to replace the SELMs with newer equipment, but National was a small operation with relatively few funds for such a capital investment.

Rather than seeing the chaos at National as simply the result of poor decision making, this analysis points to additional causes: 1) the long-term pressures of being a small subcontractor; 2) the long-term pressures inherent in American management style. I would like to examine these two forces operating, and how they each constrained specific decision making and contributed to the institutionalization of irrationality at National.

National's small scale of operation ensured that many of its production procedures were never formalized or made routine. Our lack of trained personnel, such as "methods people" found in larger industrial workplaces, exaggerated this tendency. In addition, profits and cash reserves made it difficult for management to go beyond short-term planning. Previous chapters chronicled some of the irrationalities produced by this kind of decision making. For example, it made as much sense in the long run to spend twice what they were paying me to keep an experienced mechanic—and production manager as well.

But granted National's pay schedule and recruitment procedures, they could only expect a rapid turnover of mechanics—and managers of Carroll's ability.

Subcontracting magnified these short-term pressures. There was always a fluctuating demand for our products. Workers faced the constant threat of being laid off when orders were down, and were forced to work overtime when demand was high. Also, that

Conclusions and Possibilities

National competed with companies that produced the same products kept prices and the profit margin low.

Much of the irrationality at National was the consequence of a management style that insisted on full control of all activities on the shop floor, and that saw workers' knowledge as unimportant. It embraced the iron-handed side of Taylor while ignoring the importance he granted to craft knowledge. National suffered from this attitude. The SELMs, for example, did not run ineffectively simply because National was a small shop; they ran below their potential because management held a choking grip on their control.

Perhaps the most troubling effect of working at National was that over time management's policies—in their own curious way—made sense. If one accepted the givens at National (short-term, iron-handed profit-oriented management) then the irrationalities followed quite logically. In other words, rather than being exceptions to an otherwise rational system, they instead were part and parcel of the irrational system that was institutionalized at National. From this perspective, the chaos on the shop floor was in its own way "normal." This normalization of chaos, however, is not without its costs.

The Costs of Shop Floor Chaos

A worker's perspective from the shop floor helps reveal just how damaging this chaos can be. Nearly all major problems at National, whether they concerned productivity, the quality of items, or worker discontent, are at least partly a consequence of it.

The kind of irrationality and chaos we have seen at National had the result of creating tremendous waste. Machines ran at only a fraction of their potential and produced inferior products. Materials that passed through these poorly maintained machines and ad hoc assembly procedures were discarded in vast quantities. More upsetting was the waste of human resources. As we have seen, workers' knowledge about production was systematically ignored, and to that extent degraded. The irrationality of the workplace thwarted workers' concern for quality. Although workers were neither unskilled nor uncaring about their work, the management treated them as if they were. At the same time, the chaos of the workplace rendered mere survival at National more difficult.

In a larger sense, National wasted not only workers' knowledge, but their working lives. Given the obstacles to meaningful participation, workers were left with little choice but to stop caring about their work, adopt the attitudes that management attributed to them anyway, or leave.

Possibilities and Probabilities

It is important to examine how the industrial conditions discussed here will fare in the future. I hope not so much to offer predictions as to isolate those elements that serve as preconditions for positive change.

Perhaps the first issue is the relative size of workplaces. If present trends continue, we can argue that industrial workplaces will not be growing larger; in fact, they will shrink. Furthermore, if we continue to follow the Japanese example, we can expect an increase in subcontracting and hence an increase in the number of small shops like National.

The conventional wisdom tends to see decentralization as a healthy trend. However, the resulting increase in sub-contracting

Conclusions and Possibilities

means job security and decent wages for some workers at the expense of others. Furthermore, this two-tier system does not really solve the problems of chaos and confusion, it merely hides them in small shops like National. Thus, if this present trend continues, we can only expect more shops like National and the continuation of chaos on the shop floor.

Although the relative size of the industrial workplaces is important, management style is the essential determinant of what happens on the shop floor. Indeed, we can argue from the National example that unless workers are allowed more decision making— at least over those issues that directly affect their work tasks— irrationality is inevitable. Similarly, until workers' knowledge is more fully integrated into production processes, we can expect productivity and quality to fall, despite stop-gap measures.

The future trends in management style are difficult to predict, primarily because of the numerous programs instituted in industrial workplaces under the names of "quality of worklife programs," "job humanization programs," "job enrichment programs," "quality circles," and the like, which all beg to be experiments, to one degree or another, in "workplace democracy." It is important here, however, to examine these programs in light of our "discovery" of a significant amount of chaos on the shop floor.

In many ways these programs are not new, but share in a tradition that harks to the early research of Mayo (1933) at the Hawthorne plant. Simmons and Mares' *Working Together* (1983), a summary of the various attempts at workplace democracy, elobrates on this point: "Research at Hawthorne and elsewhere demonstrated that if respect and attention were added to decent wages and pleasant working conditions, workers would be happier and therefore more productive. This work formed cornerstone for the 'Human Relations' school of management, an initial antidote to

Possibilities and Probabilities

Taylorism" (Simmons and Mares, 1983: 29). Mayo and those who followed him saw their work as an antidote to the harshness of the Taylor system. They believed that Taylor had overrationalized the workplace, and that it needed to be made more human.

Like the original Hawthorne experiment, which began by varying the level of lighting on the shop floor, many of the subsequent programs emphasize improving the environment of the workplace.[2] The more timid programs resulted in painting the walls, or the bathrooms, or piping in music to the shop floor.[3] The more adventurous implement job rotations, flex-time, and the like.[4]

I would not deny that attempts at job humanization are important to the worker. Given the conditions at National, it is difficult to oppose any attempt to improve conditions no matter how trivial. Yet given the high level of chaos on the shop floor, humanization programs do not address the basic problems which lie in production. Analyses stemming from the Mayo tradition are essentially psychological in nature: "Today's diagnosis of the 'blue collar blues' tends to psychologize even those cases of dissatisfaction and conflict that manifestly have to do with social relations and the structure of authority" (Fraser, 1983: 108). Many of the proponents of job humanization still see the problem in industrial production as overrationalization and have failed to address how irrationality and chaos may as well be involved. As long as proposed changes

2. For the link between the Hawthorne experiments and present attempts at workplace democracy, see Paul Blumberg, *Industrial Democracy: The Sociology of Participation* (New York: Schoken Books, 1968).

3. See the programs as reported in Mike Parker and Dwight Hansen, "The Circle Game," *The Progressive* 47 (January 1983): 21−27.

4. See for example Daniel Zwerdling, *Workplace Democracy* (New York: Harper and Row, 1980).

Conclusions and Possibilities

deal mainly with the psychological realm, issues of production, if considered at all, remain secondary.

There are other drawbacks to many job humanization and quality improvement programs. First, most have been instituted by management. Few have been initiated by workers or their unions. Although quality programs have been accepted by some unions, their relationship to the labor movement is tenuous at best.[5] Workers are always skeptical of the motives behind changes that emanate entirely from management.

As well, it is important to note the timing of the instituting of quality circles and many job humanization programs. As reported by Simmons and Mares (1983), the vast majority were instituted *after* a company was experiencing serious problems in productivity or quality. At least in the American experience, it seems that a company must be in serious trouble before it institutes any form of worker participation.

It is almost as if workers are the last resource that management turns to after they have exhausted all other avenues for improving quality and productivity. One has to wonder, if workers are turned to so reluctantly, how much management really values their knowledge. That quality circles commonly arise as last-ditch efforts has alarmed a number of workers as well as labor leaders. For example, Thomas Donahue, the Secretary-Treasurer of the AFL-CIO, has argued that labor did not want to become a "junior

5. Among American labor unions, quality circles have been most accepted by the United Auto Workers (UAW). A number of more progressive unions, most notably IAM and UE, are still strongly opposed. See *UE News*, July 12, 1982, pp. 3–4; and *IAM Research Report*, 10 (Winter-Spring 1982): 1–6. Interestingly enough, the more conservative AFL-CIO has taken a similar position against quality circles. See *AFL-CIO News*, January 28, 1984, p. 6.

partner in success and a senior partner in failure" (Simmons and Mares, 1983: 31).

The combination of the over-psychological emphasis combined with the timing of many quality circles and job humanization programs makes it difficult to see how from a worker's perspective they will have more than a limited success. As we have seen at National, quality and productivity are not by far simple nor superficial issues, but instead are deeply rooted in a management style that continues to grow away from an understanding of or concern with workers' shop-floor knowledge. No program, no matter how innovative or new, will be successful unless it addresses this fundamental relationship between workers and managers.

The lessons from National should be apparent. We have seen the consequences of short-term, poorly conceived programs designed to fine-tune production. Attempts to improve quality and productivity will fail unless they are welded both to production and the workers. The manipulation of people and resources by the highest level of management is not enough. Instead, it is on the shop floor that quality as well as chaos take root.

We are presently facing one of the deepest crises American manufacturing has ever seen. Hardly a segment of the American population has remained untouched by some aspect of this crisis, although clearly some have suffered more than others. Yet the knowledge and expertise we need to raise ourselves out of these difficulties lies hidden in the Alices, the Mikes, and the Ellens, as they are considered only for their hours on the job rather than for what they know. The managers in this country, at present blinded by their own schemes, possess a source of tremendous potential strength in the workers they choose to ignore. It is a source they must learn to tap before it is too late.

References

AFL-CIO. September 1984. *Workers in Jeopardy: OSHA Under the Reagan Administration.* Washington, D.C.: AFL-CIO.

———. 1984. *AFL-CIO News,* January 28, p. 6.

Aronowitz, Stanley. 1973. *False Promises.* New York: McGraw Hill.

Blauner, Robert. 1964. *Alienation and Freedom: The Factory Worker and His Industry.* Chicago: University of Chicago Press.

Bluestone, Barry, and Bennett Harrison. 1982. *The Deindustrialization of America: Plant Closing, Community Abandonments, and the Dismantling of Basic Industry.* New York: Basic Books.

Blumberg, Paul. 1968. *Industrial Democracy: The Sociology of Participation.* New York: Schocken Books.

Bogdan, Robert, and Steven J. Taylor. 1975. *Introduction to Qualitative Research Methods.* New York: John Wiley & Sons.

Borger, Robert, and Frank Cioffi, eds. 1970. *Explanation in the Behavioral Sciences.* Cambridge, Eng.: Cambridge University Press.

Bowles, Samuel, David M. Gordon, and Thomas E. Weisskopf. 1983. *Beyond the Waste Land.* Garden City, N.Y.: Doubleday/Anchor Press.

Braverman, Harry. 1974. *Labor and Monopoly Capital: The Degradation of Work in the Twentieth Century.* New York: Monthly Review Press.

Bulmer, Martin. 1985. *The Chicago School of Sociology: Institu-*

References

tionalization, Diversity, and the Rise of Sociological Research. Chicago: University of Chicago Press.

Burawoy, Michael. 1979. *Manufacturing Consent: Changes in the Labor Process Under Monopoly Capitalism.* Chicago: University of Chicago Press.

Cahn, William. 1980. *Lawrence 1912.* New York: Pilgrim Press.

Cavendish, Ruth. 1982. *Women on the Line.* London: Routledge and Kegan Paul.

Chinoy, Ely. 1955. *Automobile Workers and the American Dream.* Boston: Beacon Press.

Clawson, Dan. 1980. *Bureaucracy and the Labor Process: The Transformation of United States Industry, 1860–1920.* New York: Monthly Review Press.

Clawson, Dan, and Richard Fantasia. 1983. "Beyond Burawoy: The Dialectics of Conflict and Consent on the Shop Floor." *Theory and Society* 12: 671–80.

Cole, Robert E. 1979. *Work, Mobility, and Participation.* Berkeley: University of California Press.

Denzin, Norman K., ed. 1970. *Sociological Methods: A Sourcebook.* Chicago: Aldine.

Doeringer, Peter B., and Michael J. Piore. 1971. *Internal Labor Markets and Manpower Analysis.* Lexington, Mass.: Lexington Books.

Drucker, Peter F. 1981. *Toward the Next Economics and Other Essays.* New York: Harper and Row.

Earl, Michal J. 1981. "What Micros Mean for Managers." In *The Microelectronics Revolution,* ed. Tom Forester, pp. 356–66. Cambridge, Mass.: MIT Press.

Edwards, Richard. 1979. *Contested Terrain: The Transformation of the Workplace in the Twentieth Century.* New York: Basic Books.

References

Edwards, Richard C., Michael Reich, and David M. Gordon, eds. 1975. *Labor Market Segmentation*. Lexington, Mass.: D.C. Heath.

Forester, Tom, ed. 1981. *The Microelectronics Revolution*. Cambridge, Mass.: MIT Press.

Fraser, Steve. 1983. "Industrial Democracy in the 1980's." *Socialist Review* 72: 99–122.

Garson, Barbara. 1975. *All the Livelong Day: The Meaning and Demeaning of Routine Work*. Garden City, N.Y.: Doubleday.

Geertz, Clifford. 1973. *The Interpretation of Culture*. New York: Basic Books.

Glaser, Barney G., and Anselm L. Strauss. 1967. *The Discovery of Grounded Theory*. Chicago: Aldine.

Goffman, Erving. 1959. *The Presentation of Self in Everyday Life*. Garden City, N.Y.: Doubleday.

Goldhaber, Michael. 1980. "Politics and Technology: Microprocessors and the Prospect for a New Industrial Revolution." *Socialist Review* 52: 9–32.

Gordon, David M. 1972. *Theories of Poverty and Underemployment*. Lexington, Mass.: Lexington Books.

Gordon, David M., Richard Edwards, and Michael Reich. 1982. *Segmented Work, Divided Workers*. Cambridge, Eng.: Cambridge University Press.

Granovetter, Mark. 1984. "Small Is Bountiful: Labor Markets and Establishment Size." *American Sociological Review* 49: 323–34.

Greenbaum, Joan M. 1979. *In the Name of Efficiency*. Philadelphia: Temple University Press.

Grossman, Rachael. 1980. "Women's Place in the Integrated Circuit." *Radical America* 14: 29–50.

References

Hareven, Tamara K., and Randolph Langerbach. 1980. *Amoskeag: Life and Work in an American Factory-City*. New York: Pantheon.

Harrison, Bennett. 1982a. "Gulf and Western: A Model of Conglomerate Disinvestment." *Labor Research Review* 1: 19–23.

―――. 1982b. *The Economic Transformation of New England Since World War II*. Cambridge, Mass.: Joint Center for Urban Studies of MIT and Harvard University.

Hayes, Robert H. 1981. "Why Japanese Factories Work." *Harvard Business Review* 59: 57–66.

Hayes, Robert H., and William J. Abernathy. 1980. "Managing Our Way to Economic Decline." *Harvard Business Review* 58: 66–77.

Houbolt, Jan, and Ken Kusterer. 1977. "Taylorism Is Dead, Workers Are Not." Paper presented to the Annual Conference of East Coast Socialist Sociologist, May 28.

Howard, Robert. 1981. "Second Class in Silicon Valley." *Working Papers* 8: 21–31.

Institute for Labor Education and Research. 1982. *What's Wrong with the United States Economy*. Boston: South End Press.

International Association of Machinists. 1982. *IAM Research Report* 10: 1–6.

Judson, Arnold S. 1982. "The Awkward Truth About Productivity." *Harvard Business Review* 60: 93–97.

Junkerman, John. 1983a. "Blue Sky Management: The Kawasaki Story." *Working Papers* 10: 28–36.

―――. "The Japanese Model." *The Progressive* 47: 21–27.

Kamata, Satoshi. 1983. *Japan in the Passing Lane*. New York: Pantheon.

Kaus, Robert M. 1983. "The Trouble with Unions." *Harper's* 266: 23–35.

References

Kuhn, Sarah. 1982. *Computer Manufacturing in New England.* Cambridge, Mass.: Joint Center for Urban Studies of MIT and Harvard University.

Kusterer, Ken C. 1978. *Know-How on the Job: The Important Working Knowledge of "Unskilled" Workers.* Boulder, Colo.: Westview Press.

Leonard, Frank S., and W. Earl Sasser. 1982. "The Incline of Quality." *Harvard Business Review* 60: 163–71.

Lewis, Michael. 1978. *The Culture of Inequality.* Amherst: University of Massachusetts Press.

Linhart, Robert. 1981. *The Assembly Line.* Amherst: University of Massachusetts Press.

Lynd, Staughton. 1982. *The Fight Against Shutdowns: Youngstown's Steel Mill Closings.* San Pedro, Calif.: Miles and Weir.

Madge, John. 1962. *The Origins of Scientific Sociology.* New York: Free Press.

Magaziner, Ira C., and Robert B. Reich. 1983. *Minding America's Business.* New York: Random House.

Manwaring, Tony, and Stephen Wood. 1984. "The Ghost in the Machine: Tacit Skills in the Labor Process." *Socialist Review* 74: 57–86.

Mayo, Elton. 1933. *The Human Problems of an Industrial Civilization.* New York: Macmillan.

Melman, Seymour. 1983. *Profits Without Production.* New York: Alfred A. Knopf.

Merton, Robert K. 1949. *Social Theory and Social Structure.* New York: Free Press.

Mills, C. Wright. 1959. *The Sociological Imagination.* London: Oxford University Press.

Molony, Kathleen. 1982. " 'Contented' Labor: Selective Paternalism." *The Nation* 235: 184–85.

References

Noble, David F. 1977. *America by Design*. New York: Oxford University Press.

——. 1979. "Social Choice in Machine Design." In *Case Studies on the Labor Process*, ed. Andrew Zimbalist, pp. 18–50. New York: Monthly Review Press.

Ouchi, William G. 1981. *Theory Z: How American Business Can Meet the Japanese Challenge*. Reading, Mass.: Addison-Wesley.

Parker, Mike, and Dwight Hansen. 1983. "The Circle Game." *The Progressive* 47: 21–27.

Pascale, Richard Tanner, and Anthony G. Athos. 1981. *The Art of Japanese Management*. New York: Simon and Schuster.

Peterson, Peter G. 1982. "No More Free Lunch for the Middle Class." *New York Times Magazine*, January 17, pp. 40–41.

Pfeffer, Richard M. 1979. *Working for Capitalism*. New York: Columbia University Press.

Plewes, Thomas J. 1982. "Better Measures of Service Employment." *Monthly Labor Review* 105: 7–15.

Proctor, Nick H., and James P. Hughes. 1978. *Chemical Hazards of the Workplace*. Philadelphia: J. B. Lippincott.

Rabinow, Paul, and William M. Sullivan, eds. 1979. *Interpretive Social Science*. Berkeley: University of California Press.

Radnitzky, Gerard. 1970. *Contemporary Schools of Metascience*. 3rd ed. rev.; 3 vols. Chicago: Humanities Press.

Schrank, Robert. 1978. *Ten Thousand Working Days*. Cambridge, Mass.: MIT Press.

Scott-Stokes, Henry. 1982. *New York Times*, July 4, p. E3.

Simmons, John, and William Mares. 1983. *Working Together*. New York: Alfred A. Knopf.

Skinner, B. F. 1969. *Contingencies of Reinforcement*. New York: Appleton-Century-Crofts.

References

Swados, Harvey, 1957. "The Myth of the Happy Worker." *The Nation* 185: 65–69.

Taylor, Frederick Winslow. 1911. *The Principles of Scientific Management.* New York: W. W. Norton.

Terkel, Studs. 1972. *Working.* New York: Pantheon.

United Auto Workers. 1982. *United Auto Workers Research Bulletin,* September-October.

United Electrical Workers. 1982. *UE News,* July 12, pp. 3–4.

United States Department of Commerce, Bureau of the Census. 1949. *Census of Manufacturers.* Washington, D.C.: U.S. Government Printing Office.

———. 1977. *Census of Manufacturers.* Washington, D.C.: U.S. Government Printing Office.

United States Department of Health, Education and Welfare. 1973. *Work in America: Report of a Special Task Force to the Secretary of Health, Education and Welfare.* Cambridge, Mass.: MIT Press.

Veblen, Thorstein. 1914. *The Instinct of Workmanship, and the State of Industrial Arts.* New York: Macmillan.

Vogel, Ezra F. 1979. *Japan as Number One: Lessons for America.* Cambridge, Mass.: Harvard University Press.

Wallace, Walter. 1971. *The Logic of Science in Sociology.* Chicago: Aldine.

Weiss, Andrew. 1984. "Simple Truths of Japanese Manufacturing." *Harvard Business Review* 62: 119–25.

Wertheimer, Barbara Mayer. 1977. *We Were There: The Story of Working Women in America.* New York: Pantheon.

Wheelwright, Steven C. 1981. "Japan—Where Operations Really Are Strategic." *Harvard Business Review* 59: 67–83.

Winch, Peter. 1958. *The Idea of a Social Science.* London: Routledge and Kegan Paul.

References

Woronoff, Jon. 1983. *Japan's Wasted Workers*. Totowa, N.J.: Alanheld, Osmun.

Wright, J. Patrick. 1979. *On a Clear Day You Can See General Motors*. New York: Avon.

Zimbalist, Andrew. 1975. "The Limits of Work Humanization." *Review of Radical Political Economics* 7: 50–59.

———, ed. 1979. *Case Studeis on the Labor Process*. New York: Monthly Review Press.

Zwerdling, Daniel. 1980. *Workplace Democracy*. New York: Harper and Row.